Handbook
for Educational Secretaries
and Office Personnel

R. Carol Sweeney
Los Angeles Unified School District

Emery Stoops
Professor Emeritus
University of Southern California

ALLYN AND BACON, INC.
Boston   London   Sydney   Toronto

Library of Congress Cataloging in Publication Data

Sweeney, R   Carol, date
    Handbook for educational secretaries and office
personnel.

    Bibliography: p.
    Includes index.
    1. School secretaries—Handbooks, manuals, etc.
2. School management and organization—Handbooks,
manuals, etc.   I.   Stoops, Emery, joint author.
II.   Title.
LB2844.4.S93   371.2′023   80-25521
ISBN 0-205-07292-5

Printed in the United States of America.

Printing number and year (last digits):
10 9 8 7 6 5 4 3 2 1 86 85 84 83 82 81

Contents

iii

Preface

The Handbook for Educational Secretaries and Office Personnel is a book whose time has come. As the title implies, it is a practical guide for practicing and aspiring school secretaries as well as other interested educational office personnel. The prevailing theme is the leadership role of the educational office employee as a contributing, significant member of the educational team.

In recognition of this role, the authors have concentrated on human relations and interpersonal skills—qualities that educational office employees need and use all the time. Although the approach is unique, the information is practical. For example, the chapter on communication deals with techniques the school secretary can implement to improve the quality of the communication process between the office staff and teachers, administrators, students, and the community.

In the chapter on conflict, the authors take a realistic position in recognizing that conflict does exist in school and administrative offices; however, they take a pro-active approach in delineating methods to alleviate the problems.

The chapter on supervision provides techniques for supervising, training, and evaluating the educational office staff—techniques based on the most modern and effective methods known.

Although the focus of this handbook is on office staff members, others will also benefit from it. Administrators will learn how to build a foundation of teamwork with the office staff. Those studying to be administrators will become aware of the diverse roles of the office staff. Teachers and potential teachers will gain knowledge to enhance their interpersonal relationships with the support personnel. Students who are contemplating pursuing careers in the secretarial field will receive insight into the exciting, challenging, and rewarding job of an educational office employee.

We believe that the reader will find each chapter to be filled with explicit, workable suggestions, innovative techniques, and thought-provoking problems.

R. C. S.
E. S.

Chapter 1

The Educational Office
Employee: A Leader

Leader: One that leads, head of a group.

Webster's Dictionary

Leadership! Leadership is an extremely com
plex interpersonal relationship. If there is
no follower, there can be no leader. . . .
Leadership can only be exercised in groups
where people want to accomplish a common
goal.

Fred Fiedler

In his book *Contact, the First Four Minutes,* Leonard Zunin states
that when people meet, the first four minutes of interrelating strongly
influences subsequent contacts.

Similarly, we believe that the reader's first contact with this book
will leave a lasting impression, which will influence the reader's perceptions of each chapter read.

In this first chapter we wish to lay the foundation of the theory
that will be the common thread throughout the chapters of this book.
This link, the unifying force, is the firm belief in the school secretary as
a leader. Through this leadership, the quality of the instructional program is improved, enhanced, and enriched.

To the uninitiated, this may sound like blasphemy. Whoever heard
of the support staff, the clerks in the office, influencing the educational
program? Yet it is upon this thesis that our book is based.

Developing this theory of leadership is critical to the reader, because many of the concepts to be presented may appear at first to be
outside the realm of influence of the school secretary. This judgment is
based generally on the past stereotypes of educational office employees,

reinforced by the formal structures in most schools and offices, which give office personnel only a superficial role in running the school. However, closer scrutiny of the informal structure will generally reveal that the concept of the school secretary as a leader is widely accepted although not formally recognized.

Traditionally the school secretary is proficient in office skills: filing, typing, answering the phone, transcribing, taking dictation, composing correspondence, and organizing the office. Interestingly, surveys indicate that these skills are not mentioned when effectiveness is discussed. Informal surveys taken by the author at workshops reveal that an effective school secretary utilizes and deploys skills far beyond those listed on the job description. When school administrators describe a competent, effective school secretary, they generally extol what are commonly known as "people skills." In other words, they list communication, empathy, compassion, conflict resolution, stress reduction, and nurturing.

In addition, when pressed to enumerate specific skills needed for the job, most administrators cite responsibilities typically required of managers, such as the ability to plan, initiate, delegate, organize, implement, control, and follow a task through to completion. Furthermore, the school secretary is expected to maintain office harmony, calm demanding teachers, and soothe and allay the fears of parents.

This book was written with these qualities in mind. Instead of approaching the school office employee handbook from a stereotypical standpoint, we approach it from a real world point of view. Exactly what skills and abilities does a school secretary need to be fully effective?

Foremost is the ability to see beyond the stereotype to what is really required on the job—the utilization of all types of problem-solving skills.

Obviously such a role does not develop without the support and concurrence of the school administrator. What becomes apparent is that effective school secretaries work for effective school administrators: people who know that their own effectiveness will be enhanced by the full utilization of the resources of all personnel.

This type of school secretary is a leader who sets the tone, upholds the standards, and maintains the sense of equilibrium. In other words, this person is an integral part of the hierarchy, and the people he or she encounters in daily activities are influenced by the quality of leadership demonstrated. That influence has a ripple effect—one that usually affects everyone in the structure.

The secretary is also a leader in a changing environment. More and more educators are incorporating new behavioral science techniques into administering their schools. The technology and theories of McGregor, Maslow, Likert, Lippett, Blake and Mouton, and countless other leaders in the field of management and organization development have begun to influence the educational environment. The effective school secretary not only needs to be proficient in interpersonal skills and managerial techniques, but must also be familiar with and capable of initiating teamwork approaches and confronting conflict situations with a win/win philosophy.

Thus, the concept of leadership and the school secretary takes on a new mantle or direction: the behavioral science approach.

In each chapter of the book, the influence of the school secretary and the effect he or she has on others are discussed. Our general approach is to discuss a subject and then suggest methods and techniques to be utilized with various members of and groups in the school community, be they teachers, students, community, administrators, other office employees, or support staff. The thread is constant: practical application in the field. The message would be hollow if the applications were weak or nonexistent.

This thread is coupled with the concept of the school secretary as a leader who performs seldom recognized managerial and leadership roles. In describing the school secretary, the terms "leader" and "manager" are used with deliberation and care. Recent studies distinguish between being a manager and being a leader. An effective school secretary needs to be both.

According to studies,[1] a leader provides the initiative to go beyond the ordinary—to explore new territories, recommend new procedures, create new methods, and offer unusual remedies. A manager plans for change, coordinates efforts and resources, and implements recommended procedures.

We believe that the fully functioning, creative, effective school secretary must coordinate these two roles in a way that is supportive of administration yet stays within the legal and administrative confines of the position.

The following is a brief synopsis of how the concept of the secretary as leader and manager is applied throughout the book.

ADMINISTRATIVE/OFFICE TEAM BUILDING

In Chapter 2, Administrative/Office Team Building, the leadership role of the school secretary is discussed in relationship to the concept of

[1] James M. Lipham, "Leadership and Administration," in *Behavioral Science and Educational Administration* (Chicago: University of Chicago Press, 1964), Chap. 6, p. 125, cited in Robert G. Owens, *Organizational Behavior in Schools* (Englewood Cliffs, N.J.: Prentice-Hall, 1970).

team building. A team builder is an individual who will initiate and implement the actions required. Applying team building to the office staff is a new technique; seeing the secretary as the individual to apply this new method is even newer.

This chapter is based on techniques recommended for team building efforts of managers in industry and administrators in school. Many of the methods suggested require the school secretary to work with administration to involve school office staff in unaccustomed activities.

Suggested applications relate directly to office situations. We also recognize that the school office staff often deals with people outside the immediate office environment.

The success of Administrative/Office Team Building will be directly proportionate to the amount of leadership and managerial initiative of the school secretary.

SCHOOL OFFICE CLIMATE

School Office Climate is an extension of a term that has received a great deal of prominence in recent years. Many books enumerate countless techniques for improving school climate, but seldom is any attention given to the school office or the role of the office staff in influencing climate.

This chapter highlights the educational office employee's role in providing leadership to initiate steps for improving the working environment.

The steps enumerated, and the activities suggested, to improve school office climate may appear to be outside the traditional role of the school secretary. In effect, they are.

These steps are dependent on the leadership dimension—doing what is required by the situation. The office employee must step beyond the everyday and commonplace to respond in a creative way to the present.

Additionally, this chapter focuses on a dimension of the school that is not always seen as influencing the teachers, students, and community: the school office. The first contact with a school is probably through the office. Is this contact doing what it should? School Office Climate gives readers a new view of the school office.

COMMUNICATION TECHNIQUES FOR OFFICE STAFF

Communication is like the weather. Everyone talks about it. Yet unlike the weather, communication is an area where knowledge and techniques can have a profound effect. A skillful school secretary recognizes that communication is not only the medium; very often it is the message.

In this chapter, the various aspects of communication are addressed. What are the components of communication? How do people communicate? How does one deal with dysfunctional communication? What happens when people refuse to communicate? What about assertive communication; does it have a place in the office?

Not to be overlooked are the written communications. How can school messages convey a supportive tone? What qualities should school secretaries look for in the use of words so they are constructive, not destructive?

Coupled with the concept of communication is the leadership role of the school secretary. The educational office employee is not a passive participant. It is often up to him or her to scan written newsletters for the content and the unseen message. Oral communications must be monitored so that the office staff conveys a positive image of the school. The school secretary may want to meet with administrators and teachers to discuss how the communication process between certified and support staff often results in misconceptions and strained relationships between these two groups which are so totally interdependent.

The concepts of communication offered in this chapter are based on what research indicates is the most critical element: being "congruent" so that the words of the message and the feelings of the message are synchronized and bonded to form a total message, allowing no misunderstanding. Clearly the secretary who is a leader can be at the forefront of the effort to make feeling and message congruent. Conversely, the secretary who limits his or her role will be making a reduced contribution to the well-being of the school and office.

SUPERVISING, TRAINING, AND EVALUATING THE OFFICE STAFF

The school secretary is a pivotal person for the rest of the clerical personnel. He or she sets standards for excellence, participates in the selection of new employees, provides training for these employees, counsels and coaches staff whose performance is not up to par, and coordinates the clerical effort so that deadlines are met and offices are adequately covered. Although the supervisory role is not new to the school secretary, the techniques suggested in this chapter may be.

In this chapter, we recognize the many new methods affecting the supervision of personnel. The traditional approach is supplemented by the theories developed by McGregor, Maslow, Herzberg, Hersey and

Blanchard, and Blake and Mouton. They combine to create the innovative approaches to supervision that are now available to the office supervisor.

These authors are mentioned because the behavioral sciences have contributed immeasurably in aiding the supervisor to become a leader who recognizes the differences among people and uses this knowledge to create an environment where people have successful experiences. Closely tied to this concept is the realization that individuals have different needs at different times which should be taken into consideration in order to enhance the quality of working life.

This is clearly another facet in the multidimensional role of the school secretary who displays leadership characteristics.

CONFLICT AND ANGER IN THE SCHOOL OFFICE

To some, dealing with conflict means ignoring it and hoping it will go away. To the school secretary who accepts the leadership role, conflict is productive—a means to settle problems, restore harmony, and continue services.

A conflict may involve office staff, teachers, community—even administrative staff. It may arise out of personality clashes, communication gaps, crowded conditions, misunderstandings, or incompatibility. Whatever the cause, the secretary who wishes to alleviate the problem must take a pro-active posture. Instead of hoping the problem will go away, the school secretary must face the issue in order to see that the problem does not escalate from a minor confrontation to a major crisis.

Just as using only one method is not sufficient for training staff or communicating with people, choosing only one method to deal with conflict is also not appropriate. In a pro-active role, the school secretary must sort through the myriad of "reasons" thought to have caused the problem until the real trigger point is found.

With administrative support, the school secretary can take a dynamic lead in developing methods to turn dysfunctional conflict into meaningful growth.

A POSITIVE APPROACH TO PUBLIC RELATIONS

Think of a school secretary and the clerical staff and you think of public relations: the ability to get along with people. But under this global term there hides a job with many aspects: handling the telephone, working at the counter, dealing with the media, editing newsletters, and representing the school.

Although the role is not traditionally or formally acknowledged, the school office staff is the first line of defense of the public relations posture of virtually every school or office. Studies conducted by the National School Public Relations Association indicate that when people think of schools they think of the school secretary and office staff.

In fulfilling the responsibility of first line public relations, the school secretary's leadership role will play a significant part. The school secretary must monitor communications on the phone so that the public is treated with respect, no matter how negative a person's attitude is. In addition, it is necessary to work with administration to develop a policy regarding the media. Office staff must be trained to preserve a positive image despite pressures imposed by others. And all communications to parents must be scrutinized for typographical and grammatical errors in order to convey by deed to parents that their children's school and staff do not send anything home that would not pass the scrutiny of a knowledgeable grammarian and editor.

Accepting this responsibility places a burden on the school secretary. It is a burden that rests gracefully on the shoulders of a school secretary who acknowledges and values the role of a leader. In a time when schools are under great attack from the public and media, the school secretary who assumes this leadership mantle can be of enormous help to administration.

STUDENT WORKERS

If you, the reader, reflect on the typical junior or senior high school office and picture the people who inhabit it, you are bound to visualize students—working behind the counter, answering the phones, filing, and replenishing supplies. Student helpers are there to learn, and in the process to provide the office staff with skills, labor, and abilities.

Although the teaching and administrative staffs grade these students—legally they must—it is common knowledge that the school office staff will provide the training for these students. That the training falls to the office staff is sensible: it is the clerical worker who is knowledgeable about the switchboard, the duplicating machines, and other office functions. Yet because grading students is a function of certified staff, many office staff members feel reluctant to develop a formal training program for these students. The fear is that it may be perceived as infringing on the rights and responsibilities of the teaching and administrative staff.

Again, this is inconsistent with the leadership role of the school secretary. The effective school secretary must take the initiative in developing, with administrative support and approval, a training program for students which lies within the confines of regulations and which can tap this labor resource in a productive way.

With shrinking budgets, it is incumbent upon office staff to use every resource available. The secretary who displays and deploys leadership abilities in using student help will be providing a service to the school, the community, and, most importantly, the student.

SIGNIFICANT LEGISLATION AFFECTING THE EDUCATIONAL OFFICE EMPLOYEE

Title IX, Affirmative Action, and the Family Educational Rights and Privacy Act may seem remote to office staff. Title IX may be seen as affecting the instructional program only; Affirmative Action may be perceived as something personnel offices do in order to fulfill state and federal statutes on discrimination in hiring; and the Family Educational Rights and Privacy Act may be viewed as the province of the administrative staff. We agree insofar as the legality of each law is concerned; it is an administrative function to uphold and implement legislation. However, we believe that the educational secretary and office staff have an informal function in supporting this legislation and need to be knowledgeable about it.

For example, educational office employees should be aware of how their reactions influence those around them. The school office staff can have a powerful effect on students—staff reaction to a student who chooses a nontraditional class can be a significant factor in how that student approaches the new experience.

Additionally, affirmative action statutes do not cover just faculty. The same laws on discrimination and illegal questions are in effect when school secretaries participate in interviewing prospective members of the office staff. There are many questions that cannot be asked—school secretaries must be aware of them. Often administrators rely on the school secretaries to keep them informed of personnel policies. The school secretary must take the leadership role in this area so that the rights of employees are safeguarded.

An additional dimension involves the written communications used in schools. Although textbooks are clearly the province of the administrative and teaching staffs, the school secretary must be watchful that communications to the homes of students are scrutinized for infractions of the law.

The Family Educational Rights and Privacy Act sets specific guidelines on the handling of information pertaining to students and the delineation of who has access to records. The school office manager must develop sound records management procedures and train office staff and student workers so that this significant piece of legislation is upheld and no infractions occur.

Clearly this is a new role for the school secretary—one that leaders will fulfill with their continuing positive influence.

TIME MANAGEMENT

Just how much control does the school secretary have over the use of time? We suggest that educational office staff members, with planning and cooperation, can play a significant role in taking control of their time and making the best use of it. Time has an elastic quality that can provide flexibility to the educational secretary. Effective time management goes beyond the typical list making. In this chapter we explore time management as a dimension of several office functions.

The school secretary, in planning for effective usage of time, must take several concepts into consideration. Determining whether the office staff is morning or afternoon oriented enables one to better plan the work load. Furthermore, it is essential to make sure that time is used on tasks that are necessary to the effective functioning of the office, in contrast to tasks that are discretionary but bring enormous satisfaction to the person performing them. The school secretary who is a leader will help subordinates make this determination.

The administrative staff relies on the educational secretary to get the job done. Determining priorities facilitates this job. Lists for daily, weekly, and monthly tasks are necessary to help office staff fulfill their responsibilities.

Often valuable time is lost because of poor office setup. When looking at time usage, it is necessary to analyze desk placement and work flow. Additionally, the significance of color and its influence on time use must be considered. Finally, it seems appropriate to look at the one major task that most educational secretaries never have enough time to do—filing.

Effective time management encompasses many components. This chapter strives to suggest worthwhile, workable techniques for the educational secretary who views the job as a challenge, one that is worthy of success.

CAREER DEVELOPMENT:
A PLAN FOR UPWARD MOBILITY

We believe that a chapter on career development is a fitting component in this book.

Our unifying concept has been the leadership and managerial role of the school secretary and educational office employee. Predictably, in performing their responsibilities in an exemplary manner, educational office staff members develop skills useful in many settings.

This chapter helps the individual develop and document the experiences accumulated on the job in order to pursue other positions where these skills can be expanded.

We firmly believe that the position of school secretary is significant, meaningful, and offers opportunities for learning. We believe that our point is made by the skills, knowledge, and abilities that are developed in this position.

The techniques enumerated in this chapter will provide the reader with skills to build on the experiences gained as a member of the educational office staff.

ANNOTATED BIBLIOGRAPHY

The final section epitomizes the concept that has been a common and unifying thread throughout the book: the school secretary who is a leader recognizes the necessity to always be in the forefront of change. One must never be complacent and secure. Success as a leader is dependent on accepting that, just as education is a constantly changing field, the role of the school secretary is also changing.

Education never ends. The bibliography serves to reinforce this, for a variety of books have been annotated, books that go beyond the traditional secretarial role. The list does not support the old stereotype that the only thing secretaries do is type and transcribe. The bibliography is a testimony to the effective school secretary who displays leadership abilities.

Therefore, the books run the gamut from the traditional (typing, grammar, transcribing) to the contemporary (conflict, communications, team building, effective management, and personal growth).

The annotated bibliography is a resource for a continual beginning. The school secretary, in order to remain a leader in the educational community, must continue to seek education—education that reaches beyond the everyday for challenge, stimulation, and growth. Only through initiative and energy can one be the type of secretary that is needed: inquisitive, compassionate, ethical, and loyal.

Chapter 2

Administrative/Office Team Building

> "How can I be a member of the administrative/office team if I don't even know what the goals of the team are?"

The above is a common lament of office staff. The problem is that, to paraphrase, words do not a team make. Proclaiming that there is a team is meaningless, unless the components are present and an effort is made to develop it.

It is necessary to define exactly what the team concept is, how to determine if it is present, and what steps to take to create a climate hospitable to the team concept.

Team is not just a quality that is or isn't. It relies on a formula to exist. Examination reveals that in order for a work group to be considered a team, certain components and conditions must exist.

There must be a reason for a group to work together.
The unit must be interdependent—the members must need one another's abilities in order to reach the goals of the team.
Working together as a group must produce more than if each member worked separately.
The group must be held accountable as a unit.

Virtually all administrative and school offices pass the first test of teamness. They have a reason to work together—the educational program. They also need one another to reach educational goals. Since they rely on one another for information, working together produces more than working separately. Finally, the office is usually viewed as a total segment, not as individuals in a unit. Therefore, the qualities necessary for a team approach do exist in administrative and school offices.

The next question is to determine if these components and qualities are deployed to create a team approach. This requires closer examination and analysis. What constitutes an effective administrative/office team? According to the concepts of Reilly and Jones an administrative/office team exists when:

1. The goals of the office are clearly defined.
2. All members of the office staff have helped to establish the goals.
3. Goals are examined regularly to determine if they need to be changed, expanded, or reduced.
4. Mutual trust exists, and team members feel they can express concerns freely and openly.
5. There is recognition of the strengths and abilities of all, and efforts are made to utilize the resources members bring to the team.
6. Communication is open, and all members can express feelings openly.
7. The leadership roles are shared by all members of the office team.

Although team goals rely on a group approach, it is important to look to individual perceptions to determine if theory has been translated into practice.

Figure 2-1 may prove helpful in evaluating whether that process has taken place.

This survey can be used in several ways.

Individuals may use the survey to explore personal perceptions.
Individuals may use the survey and then share results with others in the office.
Office teams (administrators and/or members of the educational office staff) may use the survey as a planning vehicle for developing team goals for the year.

In filling out the survey, it is advisable to use two symbols and two colors of ink. With one color, the individual indicates on each scale the letter "R" for the real, everyday environment that now exists. With another color ink, the individuals writes the letter "I" to signify the ideal conditions that the individual would like to see.

If the instrument is used as a group effort, it may prove meaningful to make a composite of the group scores. In this way, everyone has the opportunity to view the whole group's idea of what is real versus what would be ideal. With this starting point, the group can begin negotiating and laying plans to reach the team ideal.

Figure 2–1 Survey on the Effectiveness of the Administrative/Office Team

As a member of the administrative/office team I (use R for Real; I for Ideal):

1. Understand the goals of the office.

   Seldom 1 2 3 4 5 Always

2. Help to determine the goals of the office.

   Seldom 1 2 3 4 5 Always

3. Participate in decisions that affect my job.

   Seldom 1 2 3 4 5 Always

4. Believe that my skills are utilized and my contribution is maximized.

   Seldom 1 2 3 4 5 Always

5. Work cooperatively with the other staff members to solve problems affecting the office.

   Seldom 1 2 3 4 5 Always

6. Practice open communications with certified and support staff without fear or anxiety.

   Seldom 1 2 3 4 5 Always

7. Am encouraged to introduce new ideas, knowing that they will be examined and evaluated fairly.

   Seldom 1 2 3 4 5 Always

8. Take an active role in the group process when leadership is shared.

   Seldom 1 2 3 4 5 Always

9. Feel confident that when issues arise my feelings will be respected and considered.

   Seldom 1 2 3 4 5 Always

10. Have a strong sense of being an integral, important member of the educational office team.

    Seldom 1 2 3 4 5 Always

After reading the chapter and performing the activities recommended, the reader is encouraged to repeat the survey to determine what, if any, changes have occurred. This activity should be repeated yearly, since outside influences and staffing changes play an important role in the team concept.

After the survey has been administered, either individually or in a group, a significant question emerges. Just what role does the secretary and office staff play in building and applying a team concept? Can a team be created if none exists? Can it be improved if the foundation is weak? And can the team be enhanced if it is already in existence, or should the school secretary leave well enough alone?

Although we may seem to be belaboring the issue, let us repeat the fundamental truth that the educational office staff members can play an enormous role in influencing the status of teamness in the office. They can explore, develop, and utilize every opportunity available to build and improve the team.

Although just knowing that the opportunity is there and developing it are quite different activities, it seems appropriate to begin by identifying and examining just what opportunities are available. There are then many techniques that can be used by a pro-active office staff to capitalize on these opportunities.

In reviewing the conditions of team that must be in effect, it becomes evident that a number of variables exist:

1. The administrative staff
2. The office staff
3. The teaching staff
4. Other members of the support staff.

It is interesting to note that the most obvious team is the one generally ignored. Ask an administrator about teamwork in the office and the response is usually "It's great!" Yet pose that same question to the office and the response may well be "What team?"

This difference demonstrates how far apart the perceptions of the administrator may be from those of the office staff.

A quick survey of books available on the team concept in education reveals an interesting phenomenon: few, if any, authors focus any attention on developing a team concept with the support staff, no less the office staff. Even when surveys and questionnaires are provided, reference to the support staff is minimal or nonexistent. Although more a sin of omission than commission, this lack of focus has created a void.

However, instead of dwelling on what is not or has not been, let us determine what steps can be taken to develop the administrative/office team.

GOAL SETTING

Often people work side by side for months and years without ever discussing what each is trying to accomplish. This condition often exists in schools and administrative offices, because time is such a precious commodity that it is difficult to set aside enough to talk, let alone discuss goals. Yet this activity is critical if teamness is to occur and flourish.

The concern might be raised whether it is appropriate for office staff to initiate a discussion on goal setting. As in other chapters in this book, we assume that these activities and suggestions are appropriate if approved by administrators.

ACTIVITY

Plan time for the clerical staff to meet with administrative personnel to discuss the development of mutual goals. Time should be set aside before or after the regular school day, and help should be sought from volunteers to cover the phones. In the event that this is not feasible, then one staff member can cover the phones with the agreement that whatever transpires at the meeting will be shared. The setting should be in a location where the group will not be disturbed (library, conference room, etc.).

Each person is given a form (Figure 2-2) on which to enumerate his/her most important responsibilities. The individual also lists what he/she perceives to be the most important responsibilities of the other side of the team. Team is defined as the administrative and clerical members of the office. It might be appropriate to have on the team one administrator and two or three clerical staff members or perhaps just one clerical person and more than one administrator. The design should meet the needs of the members of the office.

After each person has had a chance to reflect on personal perceptions of the job from the administrative and clerical points of view, the participants share their perceptions. The results are often surprising. Two people who have worked side by side for many years, assuming that they know what the other does, are often amazed by how many erroneous assumptions they have made. Sharing these lists is the first step in developing mutual goals. What may emerge is that neither one is fully aware of the scope and complexity of the other's position. It is also not unusual for an administrator to find that the secretary is deploying resources and skills in a way that does not support the overall goals of the school or office.

It is unfortunate that this type of responsibility-sharing activity seldom occurs in school offices, for this lack may place unnecessary burdens on both office staff and administration. How often does an administrator feel that a secretary is inefficient when in reality time is being spent performing jobs that the administrator is unaware of and might not even want done?

Figure 2–2

My Most Important Responsibilities	What I Believe Are Your Most Important Responsibilities

This first step in sharing job responsibilities often results in the development of a time management program. Time is allocated on the basis of real needs and priorities rather than guesswork.

OPEN COMMUNICATION

Although a later chapter is devoted entirely to communication techniques, it seems appropriate to mention here the role of open communication in the team concept. It is imperative to practice open communication in all transactions between administrative and office staff.

Often the clerical staff, through word or deed, has been led to believe that openness and sharing with administrators is inappropriate. Yet growth and improvement seldom flourish in a climate of fear or repression. The school secretary can take an assertive role in encouraging the communication process and creating an environment where concerns can be shared without fear of reprisal—an emotion not uncommon among office staff. Training in secretarial schools, compounded by a variety of experiences, often reinforces the myth that office staff should be seen and not heard. A safe, structured experience is needed to open the channels of communication.

The first exercise on job responsibilities can lay the foundation for communication. The next activity can be one of the building blocks to full and open communication.

ACTIVITY

After the group is assembled, the leader discusses the value of open communication in the school office. Since the activity of sharing may be perceived as risky, the leader should acknowledge that some may feel uncomfortable sharing. He or she should stress that growth seldom takes place without risk and that the goal of the activity is to improve the office team.

Each member of the team is then given the form shown in Figure 2-3.

Individuals reflect on their office and their team, focusing on the person with whom they interact the most. With that person in mind, they list those things the person could do to help them on the job. These may be anything—personal needs, equipment needs, communication needs, or training needs.

Then individuals should reflect on those things they would like that person to cease doing. These may be annoying behaviors, unnecessary advice, unwanted instruction—anything the other does which they believe diminishes or reduces his or her effectiveness.

The team members then share the items listed on their sheets.

The first time this activity is performed it is not unusual for the team members to share superficial concerns. Don't be discouraged. It is a beginning. As participants observe that the other members of the team do not become punitive, they will be prone to open up more in subsequent team building activities. Keep in mind that erroneous perceptions

Figure 2–3 Open Communication Activity

What I need from you is more _____

_____

_____

What I need from you is less _____

_____

_____

and stereotypes took a long time to develop and one team building activity will not diminish or eliminate them all at one time.

Caution is actually quite practical. The first time a team member hears that he or she has not been totally effective, it is natural for that individual to be demoralized. Participants should be made aware of this. Participants should also be cautioned not to be too open initially. Moderation should be the byword so that something said in haste does not come back to haunt them.

Yet, as trust develops and team members become more open in communicating their needs, this activity can prove meaningful and productive. Initial caution followed by successive steps towards openness will help build and support the team.

UTILIZATION OF MEMBER RESOURCES

Often the very element that provides structure and security to school offices becomes a significant factor in discouraging the utilization of strengths and abilities of the office staff.

A job description is admittedly crucial to providing adequate skills in an office. Generally, it is a list of skills, knowledge, and abilities office personnel must have in order to perform the job. Additionally, educational requirements are often cited to enable candidates to determine if they meet entrance requirements for the position. Yet this document often serves as an inhibiting factor when administrators see people only in terms of job descriptions and not in terms of talents they can bring to the position.

Often the list of responsibilities on the job description is seen as the top of the ladder instead of the bottom rung. Even office employees get caught in this system and do not try to utilize all their strengths, feeling that it is inappropriate to suggest that they can perform jobs outside their basic list of responsibilities. The climate of an office should encourage the discovery and use of a worker's additional skills. For example, a secretary who can design forms or write reports may remain an unknown resource in the office if a process does not exist to discover and utilize these strengths.

This syndrome of underutilization flies in the face of one of the basic tenets of teambuilding: the utilization of member resources, both traditional and nontraditional. Although this syndrome can be difficult to overcome, the team can work together to provide an appropriate climate.

Underutilization of the skills of office workers takes on an even greater significance in light of two new factors affecting the educational office. First, many school districts are facing diminished school enrollment, resulting in reduced funding. This generally culminates in reduced staff and services. However, the smaller staff usually has a work volume only slightly diminished by the reduced enrollment. The typical lament is that reduced enrollment does not reduce the number of forms or the number of interruptions. Therefore, it is critical that staff members work in an environment that fully utilizes all the strengths of the office team.

Coupled with this problem is the element of job stagnation. With the reduction of job opportunities and options for promotion, many office staff members realize that the career ladder doesn't reach too high. This demoralizing factor can be mitigated if people feel that there are opportunities for job enrichment—positions that permit the individual to bring untapped talents to the job and a climate that is conducive to employee satisfaction and exploration.

Figure 2–4   Office Employee Skill Survey

Additional skills I can bring to the position are_____

_____

_____

I would like the opportunity to develop procedures in the following areas: _____

_____

_____

Or the survey can be structured:

Please check the skills, knowledge, and abilities you possess that you wish to use on the job and currently do not have the opportunity to utilize.

____Report Writing   ____Bookkeeping
____Records Management   ____Layout

At a regular office staff meeting, present the concept of job enrichment and job expansion. Point out that utilizing skills can make the job more exciting as well as more productive. Recognize that the office staff possesses a multitude of untapped resources, some of which could be utilized on the job.

With that as a preface, a brief survey should be administered. It may take the form of open-ended questions (see Figure 2-4).

The options are endless, and the store of talent is unlimited.

Obviously, personnel practices may prohibit constantly using staff out of classification; this is not suggested or recommended here. What is encouraged is utilizing the strengths and abilities of all staff. The payoff is tremendous, especially in areas that may not be readily recognized, such as career development. For example, if an employee who is seeking better employment receives formal recognition for the performance of new duties, this can aid the individual in finding new and better job opportunities.

The utilization of the resources of the administrative-office team can only improve services to the pupils and the community, with the added inducement that it aids the individuals involved.

SHARED LEADERSHIP

Stereotypes die hard; the old image of a secretary as the person behind the scenes who makes things happen haunts the professional who now fills the position. Such a secretary may have never existed, but the myth remains that the secretary has enormous but secret powers.

As with most myths, there is an element of truth in it; however, it is so distorted it serves only to restrict the sharing of leadership with the office staff. Quite rightly, administrators are careful that their role of leader remains intact; yet modifications through sharing may prove helpful to the individual as well as the school public. Shared leadership in appropriate situations can be a fruitful democratic system. Office staff can provide input and expertise in helping determine how resources, time, and energies could be best deployed to serve the educational program.

But before pursuing this strand, let's take a look at the myth of the secretary who wields tremendous but inappropriate power, and determine how it got started and if it is still true today.

Traditionally, the secretarial role has been that of a helper, someone who is there to serve but who does not make decisions. In practice, circumstances have often altered this role. Changes in administrators create situations in which the school secretary is the only person who has information on why decisions were made and what the history of the school is. Coupled with this has been the increase in responsibilities of school administrators. As demands on their time intensified, it sometimes became expedient for administrators to turn to the school secretary for information needed to make decisions on current problems.

In many schools, this has caused a backlash. Instead of reverting to a sharing of leadership in a sensible way in areas where the school office staff has expertise, many administrators have ceased using the staff's expertise at all. That extreme, like the former, results in a loss of knowledge and involvement. It may well be up to the school secretary to reverse this trend.

Appropriate shared leadership means that in those areas where members of the team have expertise, they have an equal position in the group. Status does not inhibit contribution. Communication is free—participants do not have to censor remarks in order to make them palatable and traditional. Suggestions do not have to be channeled to one person. People feel free to comment, criticize, and share in the decisions. The resultant procedures will then be supported by all involved.

Administrators who are made aware of what the secretarial staff seeks in a shared leadership meeting will be less reluctant to participate. The school secretary is the ideal person to communicate these concepts.

If shared leadership were the norm, school office staffs would have the opportunity, as well as the responsibility, of providing input on decisions affecting their jobs. Being part of the decision-making process gives the office staff the chance to be part of the success of the project, instead of possibly being part of the failure because their valuable input was not asked for.

ACTIVITY

Request that administration meet regularly with office staff so that staff may participate in determining priorities and methods to meet deadlines.

Participate in faculty meetings as the clerical staff representative so that deadlines and workloads established incorporate clerical and teaching staff priorities.

Ask to meet with administrators and to participate, where appropriate, in decisions affecting office staff.

Encourage an atmosphere of openness at joint clerical and administrative meetings so that the office staff will not feel inhibited in sharing comments and concerns.

Share perceptions of clerical staff with administrators to make them aware of and understanding of staff needs and priorities.

INTERDEPENDENCE OF TEAM MEMBERS

At a time when people are seeking independence and self-sufficiency, striving for interdependence may seem inappropriate and incongruous. Yet interdependence is the essence of a good administrative-office team. Interdependence connotes mutual need based on specific strengths, and team members must rely on others for important strengths needed by the total team. For example, the counseling unit provides critical services to the student. But alone, without attendance procedures and textbook services, the counseling office would not be able to fully serve students. Countless other examples could be cited to illustrate this interdependence.

Another example, with an office focus, involves deadlines—often meeting deadlines in one office is dependent on receiving information from another.

This may also apply to the skills one office team member can bring to another office: i.e., form design, filing expertise, bookkeeping knowledge.

When interdependence is encouraged, it becomes the norm to view each person as part of a total unit, rather than to see people from another office as separate. This interdependence leads to synergy, a process in which two ingredients combined become greater than each separately. Then, when someone is facing a virtually impossible deadline, other team members provide help so the deadline is met. Or, if expertise in designing forms is needed, the talented member of the team, although from another office, sees the need and does not get caught up in the politics of "It's not my job."

Inherent in this process is the knowledge that individuals can pursue strengths and not focus on weaknesses.

ACTIVITY

Provide information to all team members on the relationship between offices.

Survey team members for strengths. Provide this information to all members of the team. Develop an agreement so that if a team member is needed by another unit, someone else will provide support. This prevents a strength from becoming a burden to the individual.

WORKING WITH OTHER GROUPS

When a group or team works together for a long period of time and develops in maturity, a dangerous phenomenon may occur. As the feeling of comraderie increases and intensifies, there may be a strong desire to disenfranchise all other groups and try to be a totally independent unit.

Just as interdependence of team members is critical to develop the full potential of members, it is also critical that the team work closely and cooperatively with other units. One group cannot exist in the system without the others.

For example, as members of the office teams unify with one another into one unit, the relationship with the cafeteria staff or custodial staff may become strained. The cohesiveness that serves so well in bringing the one group together serves as a barrier to keep other groups out. Additionally, relations with central offices and other support services can become strained. It may become an issue of "us" against "them."

Team members must be reminded that elitism is destructive. The same relationship should exist with other support services as within the unit.

As one office employee stated: "When I worked in a school, I always thought the people in the central office didn't know what was going on. Now that I'm in the central office, I sometimes think that the people in the schools don't know what's going on."

This, in a nutshell, is the symptom of teams not cooperating or developing support for other groups. Units can become self-centered, believing that only their goals and needs are important. It is incumbent upon the school secretary to help the team become aware of the total effort and the contributions of other school support groups.

ACTIVITY

Invite members of the central offices to visit the school, or invite members of the school to visit the central offices. Discuss with the groups the goals of each unit and how each serves the other.

Tour other units to become familiar with the working situations each experiences. In that way, people become aware of the pressures on one another and more supportive and tolerant of working environments.

Invite members of the custodial and cafeteria staffs to meet with the office staff. Become familiar with their job duties and the deadlines and pressures each group experiences. Work together to provide one another with a supportive atmosphere so that work is enhanced and good feelings between groups are increased.

A SECOND LOOK AT
ADMINISTRATIVE/OFFICE TEAM BUILDING

Team building is many dimensioned. With the multitude of facets come many complex relationships. This chapter has endeavored to make the reader aware of the many segments of team and possible activities to implement the concepts. As a culminating activity, the reader is in-

Figure 2–5   Survey on the Effectiveness of the Administrative-Office Team

As a member of the administrative/office team, I (use R for Real; I for Ideal):

1. Understand the goals of the office.   Seldom 1 2 3 4 5 Always

2. Help to determine the goals of the office.   Seldom 1 2 3 4 5 Always

3. Participate in decisions that affect my job.   Seldom 1 2 3 4 5 Always

4. Believe that my skills are utilized and my contribution is maximized.   Seldom 1 2 3 4 5 Always

5. Work cooperatively with other staff members to solve problems affecting the office.   Seldom 1 2 3 4 5 Always

6. Practice open communications with certified and support staff without fear or anxiety. Seldom 1 2 3 4 5 Always

7. Am encouraged to introduce new ideas, knowing that they will be examined and evaluated fairly. Seldom 1 2 3 4 5 Always

8. Take an active role in the group process when leadership is shared.   Seldom 1 2 3 4 5 Always

9. Feel confident that when issues arise my feelings will be respected and considered.   Seldom 1 2 3 4 5 Always

10. Have a strong sense of being an integral, important member of the educational office team. Seldom 1 2 3 4 5 Always

vited to repeat the survey on the Effectiveness of the Administrative-Office Team, using Figure 2-5. As before, the survey can be shared or used as a personal evaluation.

Did you change any of your responses?

Were you influenced by the activities?

Was your awareness raised as to the many concepts contained in the umbrella term "team"?

What changes can you institute in your team?

Does your administrator support your initiative? What can you do to provide him or her with the knowledge that his or her confidence in you will be rewarded with an improved team concept?

What techniques will you use to involve other members of the office staff in developing teamness?

How will you overcome resistance?

SUMMARY

Team building is a concept that is often used and seldom defined. We have endeavored to define it in the context of the school office, focusing on the relationships between the administrative and office team members.

Goal setting provides the base for team building, provided all members of the team are involved and the goals set are realistic.

The concept of open communication is the unifying thread in an effective team. It requires openness and trust—requisites that allow team members to share concerns openly and freely without fear of reprisals.

Team members need one another—they are interdependent. An effective team utilizes the skills and resources each member brings to it. By incorporating a process that permits each member's strengths to emerge, the entire team enhances its strengths and diminishes its weaknesses.

Shared leadership permits people to share expertise and provide guidance without thought to status or title. A natural extension of the concept of utilization of member resources, it suggests that leadership is provided by the one with the knowledge.

Finally, an effective team must be on guard against becoming so cohesive that members shun other work groups. Teams, of necessity, must be able to interface with other groups to achieve school and district goals.

The purpose of this chapter was to explore each of the dimensions of an effective team and to develop the skills needed to create such a team.

As we have said, the school secretary and office staff members are leaders, innovators, and initiators, as well as hard workers. The utilization of these skills will go a long way toward meeting the demands placed on education and educators.

PROBLEMS

Problem 1

You are the office manager of a five-person clerical staff. In the past, the feeling of camaraderie and teamness has been positive and spirits have been high.

Recently you have noticed that one of your clerks seems remote, is not friendly with other staff members, and no longer has coffee and lunch with them.

Upon investigation, you find that the clerk feels the others are taking advantage of him. As a result of being efficient and finishing work quickly, the clerk is often asked to help the others. Although reluctant to do so, the clerk feels unable to refuse.

Other staff members (and teachers and administrators) have also noticed that the clerk is quiet and withdrawn.

As the office manager, what team building activities would you conduct to alleviate the problem and restore the team spirit?

Over what period of time would you conduct these activities?

Would you involve administrators?

What other steps would you take?

Problem 2

As a new secretary, you are reluctant to make waves. Yet you find that people who work in the office do not cooperate with one another. Each office is autonomous and meets deadlines without outside help.

In the past, you have been committed to the team concept. You would like to institute some changes.

Although the principal seems receptive to your ideas that office members should help each other, she seems to resist team building activities.

What do you do?

Problem 3

You are used to working alone. In the new office everyone seems friendly and wants to cooperate with you. As the new secretary, you don't know which way to turn.

How do you handle the changed environment?

Problem 4

Members of two offices have been feuding. Each group feels its work should take precedence over the other's and will not pitch in to help the other group when it faces pressing deadlines.

As the school secretary, what steps would you take to alleviate the problem?

Problem 5

As secretary to the superintendent, you are often confronted by school secretaries who feel that your staff does not understand the pressures in an individual school. Since you have never worked in a school, you feel at a loss to smooth feelings or remedy the situation.

Recently your boss called you into the office to discuss the poor relationship. He asked you to develop a plan to improve relations with school office staffs.

What steps do you take?

Bibliography

Beckard, Richard. *Organization Development: Strategies and Models.* Menlo Park, Calif.: Addison-Wesley, 1969.

Lippitt, G. L. *Organizational Renewal.* New York: Appleton-Century-Crofts, 1969.

Owens, Robert G. *Organizational Behavior in Schools.* Englewood Cliffs, N.J.: Prentice-Hall, 1970.

Reilly, Anthony, J., and Jones, John E. "Team-Building," in *The 1974 Annual Handbook for Group Facilitators.* LaJolla, Calif.: University Associates, 1974, pp. 227–237.

Solomon, Lawrence N. "Team Development: A Training Approach," in *The 1977 Annual Handbook for Group Facilitators.* LaJolla, Calif.: University Associates, 1977, pp. 181–193.

Chapter 3

School Office Climate

School climate is a subject that has been generating a great deal of interest lately. Administrators recognize that environment plays a significant role in contributing to the quality of education. Classrooms, auditoriums, lunchrooms, and athletic fields are examined to determine their positive and negative influences on the student. Staff is evaluated and trained to enhance learning by creating an environment conducive to education. In the process of evaluating the school environment, educators have overlooked a significant location: the school office. Since it is not perceived as a traditional classroom, administrators have tended to bypass this area when conducting surveys on the school atmosphere. Incredibly, even office staff members have overlooked their own territory while serving on school committees whose sole purpose is to "improve the school climate."

This chapter focuses on the school office as a significant factor in determining the total school climate. Whether it is an enhancing or detracting factor is an area to be explored and measured. The question must be asked: What efforts are being made to fully utilize every element available in the school office to contribute to the quality of education?

DISCOVERING YOUR OFFICE CLIMATE

As a first step, the reader is invited to use the following personal survey (Figure 3-1) to develop his or her own perception of the office climate. Giving the survey to other members of the school staff and community, if appropriate, will validate personal perceptions and also provide a composite profile of how others view the school office. The results of the survey can be used to make definite, achievable plans for improving office climate to convey the fact that the school office is part of the total school effort.

Figure 3–1   School Office Climate Survey

1. When visitors walk into the office they are greeted warmly.   Seldom 1 2 3 4 5 Always

2. Staff members from other offices feel welcome.   Seldom 1 2 3 4 5 Always

3. Teachers appear to be comfortable when entering the office and are not reluctant to ask for help.   Seldom 1 2 3 4 5 Always

4. Students seem confident of being served.   Seldom 1 2 3 4 5 Always

5. Administrative staff members are treated fairly, but are not fawned over or treated differently from others.   Seldom 1 2 3 4 5 Always

6. Community members seek help from all staff members, not just a few.   Seldom 1 2 3 4 5 Always

7. Parents comment on the pleasant atmosphere and the feeling of service and support they receive from the office staff.   Seldom 1 2 3 4 5 Always

8. Bulletin boards are topical and are changed regularly.   Seldom 1 2 3 4 5 Always

9. Seats are available for students, staff, and visitors.   Seldom 1 2 3 4 5 Always

10. Cafeteria and custodial staffs are made to feel welcome when they enter the office.   Seldom 1 2 3 4 5 Always

11. Phones are answered in a pleasant manner, and information is dispensed in such a way that inquirers are not reluctant to call back.   Seldom 1 2 3 4 5 Always

12. People walking into the office are acknowledged immediately and do not wait to be served.   Seldom 1 2 3 4 5 Always

13. An overall evaluation of the school office climate is   Low   1 2 3 4 5 High

On the rating scale, did your office come up as "the dungeon"? Or were you rewarded with a comment such as this one, by a school secretary: "The atmosphere is one of warmth and support, people are nice, and the feeling of those crazy grinning faces prevails. You can't help smiling because everyone smiles at you." If the survey reinforced a view of the school office as a positive factor, then the question is how to continue and enhance what is already in effect. If the survey indicated that the office climate is not all that could be expected, the next step is to determine what can be done to change the image.

Whatever the results of the survey, the next step is to get to specifics. "Feeling good" is judgmental, personal, and hard to measure. Yet most evaluations tend to describe climate in terms of people, people qualities, and people skills. Even when inanimate objects, such as bulletin boards and buildings, are being described, personal characteristics seem to emerge. However, if we wish to improve office climate, we must be specific in what behavior should be changed, eliminated, or added.

Given that school office climate is difficult to quantify, let's look at different ways school office climate is demonstrated.

Students: Students enter the office and feel welcome. Office staff members are courteous and serve students as readily as they do staff. Adult students are treated with dignity and do not feel intimidated by the staff.

Other Support Personnel: Members of the support staff (custodial and cafeteria) feel comfortable upon entering the office. They are greeted by name and feel welcome.

Teachers: Teacher needs are addressed fairly and impartially. The feeling of comraderie is evident. All share a common goal: the education of the students.

Parents: Parents perceive the school office as a place where questions are answered and they are welcomed, no matter what their concerns. Staff is trained to deal with problems without conveying anger or impatience to the parents.

Community: The school is a place where community members may enter and feel welcome, whether they have students attending or not. Concerns and complaints are handled with courtesy.

Administrators: All members of the administrative staff feel welcome in every office. Services are equitable, yet office staff views emergencies and priorities as a team and works cooperatively to meet deadlines. Additionally, members of central office staff see the school office staff as warm, supportive, and efficient. The relationship between staffs is one of mutual respect and shared concerns.

STEPS TO BUILD, IMPROVE, ENHANCE, AND REFINE CLIMATE

Accepting the qualities listed in the previous section as criteria by which a sound school office climate is measured, the reader is still faced with the following questions: "Just what can educational office employees do to initiate and implement change? Aren't many of the qualities listed the province of administrators? Would it be inappropriate if office staff engaged in activities aimed at improving, changing, or enhancing the office climate?"

Obviously, nothing can be achieved and no change embarked upon without the total consent and support of administration. Yet experience indicates that educators appreciate a show of interest by the school office staff in improving this important segment of the school environment. Therefore, the suggestions that will follow are offered for the school secretary or office staff member who not only desires to improve office climate, but also has the support of administration to do so.

STUDENTS IN GENERAL

Often the best barometer of school office climate is the perceptions students have of the school office and its staff. This can be measured by the students' willingness to go to the office either to seek information or to convey messages from teachers.

Although administrative policy and procedures establish the frequency and reasons why students enter a school office, the secretarial staff plays a significant role in how welcome the student feels.

As one student aptly described it: "When I go into the main office, I feel as if I really count. They know my name and smile at me and I don't feel as if I had two heads, no matter how dumb my question is."

Following are suggestions for improving or enhancing student perception of the school office climate in your school.

ACTIVITY

Try to greet students by name. Although in large schools this may be difficult, addressing someone by name is a real indication that you care. If that's impossible, a broad smile makes up for the lack of name knowledge, and a friendly "Hello" also creates a pleasant feeling.

Now this technique may seem simplistic, unless you reflect that encounters with students happen literally hundreds of times a day, and keeping that smile fresh and genuine may call for superhuman powers.

Conveying a warm school office climate is commendable, but no one ever said it would be easy.

ACTIVITY

Student workers provide an important service to the school while receiving credit for their experiences in the office. Although the student reports directly to a certified member of the staff (who is responsible for the student and the grading), the educational office staff plays an important role in the student's experience in the office. Therefore, it is incumbent upon the office staff to provide an environment that will support the educational goals determined by the administration.

Office staff can enhance learning by providing meaningful duties for students to perform. This includes providing the training for the duties as well as explaining the significance the job has to the school.

Although providing training may be the duty of a certified teacher, the office staff may best provide actual experience in office skills. Therefore, office staff members must be aware that their attitudes and behaviors are influencing the student's perception of the office. Staff members must also be aware that school office climate is directly affected by how they handle this responsibility. Chapter 8 will discuss in detail methods of working with student workers within the confines of administrative policies and procedures.

ADULT STUDENTS

Recognition must be made of a new category of student, the mature adult. For those office staffs working in schools where the mature adult is a student, efforts must be made to ensure them the same measure of acceptance as is given to the traditional student.

Often the older student is returning to school after a lengthy hiatus. The individual may be uncertain of skills or feel intimidated by the size of the school plant and the number of people who seem intent on a purpose. Mature students can feel isolated and alienated. And, typically, the office is the first place they go, an oasis of sorts. Here the educational office staff can play a significant and meaningful role. The self-esteem of the mature student may be fragile, he or she may be reluctant to ask for help, and, most important, he or she may feel rejected if not treated carefully.

A friendly word may be all that is needed to allay fears; conversely, a frown may be all that is needed to confirm that the adult student doesn't belong there, and he or she may flee, perhaps never to return.

ACTIVITY

There are many ways the educational office staff can ease the transition of the mature student. As stated, friendliness and patience lead the list. Yet there are a few areas that may be overlooked.

Many mature students have failing eyesight. Forms should be typed with pica or larger type to enable students to read the material unaided. Also, help should be provided for those who need assistance in deciphering forms and applications. Those of us in education, no matter what level, become accustomed to lengthy forms and complicated terminology. A mature adult may find it difficult to ask for help, yet feel rejected if none is offered. The educational office staff must take the initiative.

Hearing loss may also be a problem to the mature adult. Office staff must recognize this possibility so that such a student will receive additional services and help, if required.

STUDENTS WITH DIVERSE ETHNIC BACKGROUNDS

More and more, the educational office staff is being called upon to serve students with diverse ethnic backgrounds. It is essential that steps are taken to ensure their smooth transition into the school. The following activities can be explored and planned if administrators concur.

ACTIVITY

Learn commonly used phrases and sentences in appropriate foreign languages in order to communicate more effectively with students who speak English as a second language.

ACTIVITY

Extend support and assurance to students who are new to the school and who have come from an area or country where customs are different. Their first encounter with the school will probably take place in the school office with the office staff. Make that first impression positive and helpful. Walk up to the counter to greet them. Explain registration and school procedures. Encourage them with smiles and positive gestures. If appropriate and available, offer foreign language translations.

OTHER SUPPORT PERSONNEL

Physical distance and different job responsibilities often combine to form barriers between office personnel and other support staff. These barriers can create an atmosphere of distrust which leads to poor communication. Although theoretically each group has the educational program as its common goal, in practice each may view its territory and responsibility as more important than others. The school office staff can play a significant role in reducing these barriers and opening up the communication process.

ACTIVITY

Extend a feeling of welcome to all support staff who come to the office. Greet them with respect—this models the type of behavior that will be expected from students and other members of the staff.

School custom should dictate whether support staff members are addressed by first name or Mr., Mrs., Miss or Ms. Keep in mind that if certified staff is addressed by Mr., Mrs., Miss or Ms. and support staff by first name, a double standard is created, one that may convey the message that one group is worthy of more respect. Although this may not be the intent, it could be so perceived by students and staff.

ACTIVITY

At the beginning of each school year, meet with the plant manager, cafeteria manager, and other supervisory support staff to determine what office services will be needed throughout the year. This may include typing, payroll, supplies, etc. By establishing needs and priorities, office staff can provide services at other than peak times and yet fulfill the needs of the support staff. Thus, by word and by deed, the office staff conveys to other support staff members that it respects their contribution and welcomes them as part of the educational family.

Additionally, by providing this service it delivers a far more meaningful message to support staff: we believe that you provide services to this school and are entitled to the same quality of service that other staff members are. In addition, you are entitled to it in a manner that supports your meaningful contribution to the school.

This posture has enormous significance. Since sometimes the value of all support personnel (including the office staff) is not recognized, it is crucial that the educational office staff model the type of behavior that they wish all people (certified staff as well as others) to receive.

SUBSTITUTE OFFICE WORKERS

Often districts provide for clerical substitutes when regular office staff members are ill or away. The services these substitutes provide range from filling in for the absent employee to just "filling a desk."

The quality of the services provided, obviously, is dependent on the skills of the individual. But there are many ways in which the regular office staff can enhance the performance of the substitute.

ACTIVITY

Provide all clerical substitutes with a "Sub" folder. In it have lists of faculty and support staff, with telephone extensions and room numbers. In addition, if possible, include a composite of snapshots of staff so that names and faces are easier to match. These snapshots may be copied from the display of faculty and staff photos in the main office, if there is such a display, or they may be taken from the yearly photographs shot for the school.

Another essential item for the substitute is the bell schedule for regular and special events. Often the substitute is in the office alone and cannot turn to anyone for help. The folder should also contain a compilation of information necessary to perform the job.

ACTIVITY

Provide a "buddy" system for clerical substitutes. Any new person on campus is likely to feel isolated. The feeling may be intensified if the individual knows that the assignment will probably be for only a short period of time. Going out for coffee break and lunch with another member of the office staff serves many purposes. The substitute has the opportunity to: ask questions and gain valuable information; become familiar with the campus; and, most important, have a feeling of belonging —a feeling that is bound to improve relationships with everyone on campus. Obviously, an enhanced perception of the school will have a positive effect on the school office climate.

TEACHERS

Teachers often measure school office climate in terms of tangible items: supplies, typing, telephone messages. This is not because people and attitudes are unimportant; rather, it is because tangible items are the lifeblood of the classroom.

Office staff are often faced with the dilemma of striking the happy medium: service without servitude. Providing supplies for teachers when reports are due often taxes the most dedicated office staff. Unexpected typing wreaks havoc when several teachers are pressing for immediate service and administrators are depending on those same clerical personnel. With this sort of pressure, a genuine smile often turns to a frozen grin.

The National Association of Educational Office Personnel coined an expression that seems an appropriate motto for the professional school office staff: "Don't panic, adjust." And adjust translates to "Plan ahead."

ACTIVITY

Since often the need for last-minute supplies creates pressure on the school office staff, developing a process for making those items available can be the first step in reducing pressure.

A bookshelf in the main office is one solution. Stock the bookshelf with unlimited, inexpensive supplies that teachers commonly need: pencils, pens, memo papers, paper clips, newsprint, foolscap paper, and other items appropriate to your school. At a staff meeting, inform the teachers that these items are available to them at any time and they are free to "shop" at this store any time they are in the office. Student workers can be trained to replenish the supplies. Request teachers not to hoard, and indicate that every effort will be made to maintain a plentiful supply. When teachers realize that this source is always available, they will not have to bother office staff for routine items.

Concurrent with the introduction of the supply bookcase, introduce another procedure whereby more expensive supply items are requisitioned. Obviously this system must be amenable to the school policy. If different departments control specific budget amounts for the teachers, the system must be developed to coincide with, and not contradict, existing policies. By establishing a climate of support through the inexpensive supply route, office staff will find it easier to gain the cooperation of teachers on major purchases.

The ordering of more expensive supplies and equipment can be an easy process if the office staff provides the forms and procedures. The use of the form illustrated (Figure 3-2) will give the clerical staff all the data they need to place the order as well as provide the teachers with information on delivery date. The form can be produced on NCR (no carbon required) paper and made out in triplicate. One copy is retained by the office, one copy is returned to the teacher, and one copy is given to the plant manager so the receiving room staff will be aware of who ordered the article. Delivery can then be made to the appropriate individual as soon as an item is received.

Please note that the form provides for the department chairperson (if appropriate) and the principal to approve the order, if necessary. Thus, a check and balance system is maintained.

Figure 3–2   Order Form for Supplies or Equipment

Teacher's Name   Date   Department

                                                      Department
                                                      Approval

---

                                                      Principal Approval

Supply/Equipment   Item #_____   Date Needed_____
Needed (describe
fully):

RETURN TO TEACHER

---

name

Your order has been received. Tentative date for delivery is _____.

Your order will be held till _____, our next ordering date. Tentative date for delivery is _____.

Item is out of stock. Tentative delivery date is _____.

The item is no longer available. Please check with office staff on alternative items.

Original (white)—office staff
Duplicate (green)—custodial staff
Duplicate (pink)—teacher

Providing typing and duplicating services poses a difficult problem for the office staff. Often deadlines coincide and clerical staff is overtaxed trying to meet the crisis adequately. Here again, the use of office forms provides a structure for accommodating the needs of both teachers and office staff.

At the beginning of each semester, meet with the teaching staff to discuss clerical needs. Inform teachers about typical deadlines and peak office times. Often teachers are completely unaware of the variety of forms, deadlines, and outside pressures on the educational office staff. Sharing this knowledge with them will help them understand and be part of the solution, rather than part of the problem. Often what is viewed as insensitivity and unconcern is merely lack of knowledge.

After presenting office staff needs to the teaching staff, introduce a forms system. Using this system, work to be done is accompanied by a request form (Figure 3-3) giving pertinent instructions on the material needed. This information should document needs as well as time constraints. Office staff can then form priorities in work, and certified staff will have a reasonable chance of receiving the work on time. A tray can be provided on a counter so that teachers can drop their work off.

Students can be trained to use duplicating machines to run off the material. In addition, advanced typing students can be trained to prepare work for duplication. With the cooperation of the business education teacher, outstanding students can be used as capable typists and office helpers. Students receive experience, and clerical staff gets help. Obviously, this must be within the constraints of the educational program and cannot be contrary to personnel rules.

ACTIVITY

One method of conveying a feeling of welcome to teachers is to set up a bulletin board displaying pictures of staff members. These photographs can also help both parents, who may come in to see a teacher whom they have never met, and substitute clerical staff and teachers, who often spend days on campus without knowing the names of other staff members. The pictures can be tacked to a cork board or foam panel. Pictures can be either snapshots provided by the teacher or the standard school pictures taken yearly.

The bulletin board can be used to highlight the different departments in the school and the certified or support staff who work there. Birthdays can be acknowledged. A strong feeling of family results from

Figure 3–3   Typing and Duplicating Request Form

Teacher's Name   Date Requested   Date Needed

Quantity needed _____

Number of pages submitted _____

Retain master _____Yes

_____No

Assembling instructions: Staple pages _____

Two-sided copy _____

Paper instructions: Color _____

Weight _____

3-hole punch _____

Typing instructions: Single-spaced _____

Double-spaced _____

Special type _____

Other instructions_____

_____

_____

treating the people who come into the office as individuals. Here, too, the consent and support of administration is necessary.

PARENTS AND COMMUNITY MEMBERS

If education is the product and the student is the customer, then it is not difficult to see parents and community members as contributors to the product—both as taxpayers and as supporters. Yet, often the public sees the school as merely a large edifice—a faceless entity. The school office staff can alter this perception, as shown by a recent study by the director of public relations in a midwestern city.[1] When parents were asked to name the person they know who works at their local school, the person most often cited was the school secretary. This perception does not diminish the importance of other staff members; it merely confirms and reinforces the significance of the school secretary or office staff member.

Office staff members must recognize their prominence in the eyes of the public and use it to best advantage. If the public turns to the office staff first, then the office staff must develop skills that will create a positive image.

Thus, in addition to the others they serve—students, teachers, administrators, and other support staff—the office personnel must also serve parents and community members. Providing this additional measure of service could tax the most dedicated employee. Therefore, care must be taken that this important segment of the school public receives sufficient attention without causing other services to be reduced or neglected. In the segment on teaming and office techniques, problems of and questions on working with the public will be addressed.

ACTIVITY

Recently the nation was bombarded by the silly "smile" symbol— a round toothless face with a silly grin. It was difficult to look at this face without grinning. These little plastic disks can do wonders when affixed to the base of a telephone; they are a constant reminder to the clerical staff to smile.

It is not always easy to smile when pressures are accelerating. However, the public is probably completely unaware of the pressures. Without denying that smiling may well be the last thing you want to do,

[1] Study conducted by John Wherry, currently Executive Director of the National Public Relations Association, when he was director of Public Relations for the Kansas City Public Schools.

remember that it may well prevent another problem from occurring: a complaint by an angry parent who feels that he or she was not treated warmly or fairly by the clerk who answered the phone.

ACTIVITY

Make a concerted effort to respond to and serve people who come to the counter. Even if you are on the phone and cannot get up immediately, acknowledging the person conveys the message that he or she is important.

If necessary, rearrange office furniture and desks so that at least one person is facing the counter. If this is not feasible, a little ingenuity may save the day. We knew an educational office employee who positioned a rear-view mirror on the desk and installed a concave mirror near the ceiling. Then when she was engrossed in typing she could still monitor the counter. And if she were in the supply or duplicating room and could not see the counter, she could maintain indirect eye contact through the use of the mirror.

In addition, provide a bell for visitors to ring. In that way visitors know that although the office is empty, someone will be within earshot and will respond to a ring.

ACTIVITY

Keep bulletin boards updated with current events at the school to apprise parents and community members of educational activities. To give the office staff latitude in developing creative bulletin boards, plan with administrators on appropriate material at the beginning of the school year so that it is not necessary to turn to certified staff for constant approval.

An additional note: if the student body is multicultural, be sure that the bulletin board reflects the ethnic diversity of the community.

ACTIVITY

Provide maps of the school for visitors. If appropriate, send a student to escort newcomers on the school grounds.

PARENT-TEACHER ASSOCIATIONS OR SCHOOL ADVISORY COUNCILS

The PTA has long been an important contributor to education. This relationship with the school system can be greatly enhanced by the school office staff. In addition, in many communities throughout the country, school advisory councils have been formed which may have activities similar to or different from those of the PTA. Here, too, school office staff is usually the first contact these school support associations have with the local school. The quality of the service provided, as well as the manner in which this service is administered, plays an important role in the perception these groups have of the educational program.

With the press of normal office activities, it would be understandable if educational office employees viewed these groups as just one more segment of the public to be served. However, if the staff develops a systematic way to provide services to these groups, this will prevent overtaxing of the staff's time or abilities.

ACTIVITY

Meet with the PTA or advisory committee leaders at the beginning of the fall semester to determine if they anticipate a need for office services throughout the year. In working with the administrative staff to facilitate this meeting, the school office staff can accomplish two goals: one is to make the PTA or other association aware of the work load facing the office; and the other is to involve administration so they too can serve as a buffer for unreasonable demands from outside groups. In addition, the supportive administration will be more reluctant to agree to fulfilling the association's requests without first checking with the office staff.

In the process of exploring the needs of both groups, the school secretary can develop a calendar so that peak loads in the office are accommodated without slighting association needs.

ACTIVITY

If permitted by district and administrative policy, train parent volunteers to run duplicating machines so they can provide for the needs of the association. This may serve another purpose—often a well-trained volunteer becomes part of the office staff. This training is often an investment in the clerical staff of the future.

ACTIVITY

Become involved in association activities to become better acquainted with community members.

COMMUNITY VOLUNTEERS

Community volunteers working with students in classrooms have become a familiar sight on many campuses. Their presence can make a significant contribution to the quality of education.

Often, as part of their duties, they type and duplicate materials for teachers, thus coming in contact with office staff. Because they often need help and training in office procedures, there is a danger that volunteers could be viewed in a negative light by the office staff, resulting in their being treated in a less than exemplary fashion. Obviously this does not add to the image of a positive school office climate. Since the services volunteers provide have become such an important part of the educational process, office staff should structure use of the volunteers' expertise and provide appropriate training.

ACTIVITY

Give volunteers a tour of the office to acquaint them with the location of supplies often requested by the teachers. The volunteer can then fill orders without bothering office staff.

ACTIVITY

If permitted by law and personnel policies, train volunteers on methods of duplicating material.

ACTIVITY

Inform volunteers of hiring practices. They, like the Parent-Teacher Association members and community council members, often look to the schools for employment. The volunteer you train could be an investment in future office staff.

ACTIVITY

Refrain from speaking about others in front of volunteers or community members. Remember, they may misinterpret something that is said, and create a poor image of the school because of this misinformation. Additionally, before permitting volunteers or community members access to offices, familiarize yourself and other office staff with federal, state, and local laws pertaining to the release of information regarding students. The assumption should not be made that office staff is totally aware of all the dimensions and ramifications of the privacy laws. Clarification with administration will prevent any abridgment of anyone's rights.

ADMINISTRATIVE STAFF

When the dynamics of school office climate are being explored, there is a real danger that the administrative staff members could be overlooked. Because they are part of the everyday environment, this important segment of the office family may be taken for granted. One might assume, erroneously, that if the school office climate was not as they wished, they, of all groups, would do something about it. Actually, administrative staff members may have grave concerns about the school office climate, but, because they work in such close proximity to support office staff, they may feel a reluctance to broach the subject.

Administrators may also have so many demands from the educational program that they leave the school office climate in the hands of the school secretary and hope for the best.

Therefore, it is critical that the school office staff and school secretary take the lead in providing a school office climate supportive of the efforts of the administrative staff.

ACTIVITY

Request a meeting with members of the administrative staff and ask them for specific feedback on their perception of the climate in the office. This may be done through the personal survey in the beginning of the chapter or it may be done through a series of questions, such as:

1. Do you feel welcome when you walk in each office?
2. Is the method used to answer the phone one you like, or do you have any changes to suggest?
3. How do your colleagues feel when they visit the school offices?
4. When you call the office when out in the field, does our tone convey warmth and service?
5. What suggestions do you have about the bulletin boards and general environment of the office?
6. What recommendations would you make to the school office staff to enhance the school office climate?

By taking the initiative and requesting this input, the school office staff removes the burden from the administrators while demonstrating that the staff is open to suggestions.

SUMMARY

In the past, the concept of school office climate was either ignored or glossed over. Yet it is clear that the attitude of this important segment of the school plant can either contribute greatly to or diminish the overall pleasantness of the environment of a school.

As a school office employee, you must take the lead in exploring the dynamics of the office climate. This can be handled in a variety of ways. Following are goals to keep in mind:

Students should perceive the office as a friendly place, one where they are treated with dignity and receive the help they need.

Other support staff should feel welcome and comfortable when they enter the office.

Teachers need to know that the school office is a place of service to them, one that supports them in their role as educators.

Parents should view the school office as a place where they can find acceptance and get answers.

Community members must be able to see the school as an institution of integrity and service.

Finally, administrators need to know that the school office is an efficiently run entity which contributes significantly to the well-being of the student body and staff.

The activities listed in this chapter are only a beginning. With imagination, clerical staff can develop a multitude of techniques to achieve these goals.

PROBLEMS

Problem 1

A new elementary school is to be opened, and you have been selected to be the school secretary. Three clerical personnel have been selected, and you are having a meeting to plan for the opening of the school. Your goal is to establish a school office climate that will convey a feeling of warmth, support, and service to people who enter the office.

What steps can you take to convey this to teachers, support personnel, parents; students, community, and administrative staff?

Problem 2

Mary Jones was visiting her neighborhood school when one of the clerks became very irritated and was rude to her. Mary is a school secretary at a nearby school, but she did not reveal that to the clerk—she just left.

At a subsequent meeting at the administrative offices, the school secretary recognized Mary and asked her about the incident. Mary brushed it aside and told her it was nothing.

How do you think Mary should have handled the original situation?

Do you approve of the way she is handling it now?

Problem 3

Members of a minority group have recently moved into the community. The principal has asked you and your clerical staff to recommend ways to welcome these new members of the community.

How can you make the school office more inviting?

What techniques can the office staff implement that would make minority members feel more welcome?

Bibliography

Ferguson, Donald; Rowson, Joseph; and Marx, Gary. *Making the Wheels Go Round in School Public Relations.* Arlington, Va.: National Schools Public Relations Association, 1975.

Fox, Robert S.; Schmuck, Richard; Van Egmond, Elmer; Ritve, Miriam; and Jung, Charles. *Diagnosing Professional Climates of Schools.* Fairfax, Va.: NTL Learning Resources Corporation, 1975.

Jones, Florence Glenn. *How to Run a More Efficient School Office.* Englewood Cliffs, N.J.: Prentice-Hall, 1966.

Robert, Marc. *School Morale: The Human Dimension.* Niles, Ill.: Argus Communications, 1976.

School Climate Improvement: A Challenge to the School Administrator. Bloomington, In.: Phi Delta Kappa, 1974.

Chapter 4

Communication Techniques
for Office Staff

"Gee, Mrs. Jones, it's so nice to come in here. You always have such a nice smile."

"I really appreciate the way you give me instructions. They are always so clear."

"When I hear your voice on the other end of the phone, I always feel that I'll get some help."

"Mr. Smith, I certainly appreciate your openness. You share your concerns in such a supportive way. It helps us to work together more productively."

Communication is many-faceted. For educational secretaries and office personnel, communication is the one factor critical to the well-being and effectiveness of the office. If the communication process works, nobody notices it. If it does not work, everyone knows that something is wrong. However, the communication process is not always recognized as the culprit; instead, there may be vague references to an unfriendly atmosphere, a cold office, or a staff that is always rushed. People may avoid going into the office unless they must. And students may seem to be in a hurry to get in and get out. Only careful analysis will reveal that a problem such as people avoiding the office is caused by the fact that the communication gap has increased into a chasm.

The school secretary and office personnel have a vital role in the communication process of the school and office. Their role and the dynamics of communication will be explored in this chapter.

THE ELEMENTS OF COMMUNICATION

In an informal workshop survey, educational office employees were asked what one thing took most of their time. Without hesitation they responded: "Serving people, either on the phone or in person, communicating with others."

Recent studies support their conclusions. People spend approximately 70 percent of their waking hours engaged in interpersonal communication. This 70 percent is further classified as

9 percent writing
16 percent reading
30 percent talking
45 percent listening.

The significance of these figures cannot be overlooked when one is analyzing the responsibilities of the office staff. With over 70 percent of a school secretary's time spent in interpersonal communication, it is crucial that the process be clear, concise, and without misunderstanding.

Just what is communication? We've discussed the time that people spend in communicating, but just what is the vehicle?

WORDS

Words are the foundation of most communications. Yet words offer the potential for misunderstandings. For example, mention the word "dog" and many people think fondly of their pet and the pleasure and safety the animal brings to the home. Yet mention "dog" to someone else and the person conjures up a vision of a snarling animal, ready to bite. The person's past experience with dogs was undeniably unpleasant. Still another person hears the word and thinks of the verb dog, as in "he dogs his very steps." And yet another thinks of the slang expression used to describe a person who is not liked.

It is easy to see why words, although our basic tools of communication, create erroneous images or misinformation.

NONVERBAL COMMUNICATION

Body language is a medium for communication. Many books have been written to help people decipher messages people are conveying through their gestures, facial expressions, posture, and social distance (how close they stand to you).

The danger lies in accepting the translations as being absolute, without exploring other messages hidden behind the gestures. For example, someone who frowns and looks skeptical may well be weighing some information. Or, just possibly that individual is trying to focus without glasses, or has a hearing problem. A person who stands close to the communicator may be trying to move into his or her space, may simply have a hearing problem, or may have been raised in a country where people stand close to others.

Certainly use and interpretation of nonverbal communication is one more tool office personnel need to correctly evaluate communications in the school office.

EMOTIONS

Recently, writers have started to focus on the feelings that people transmit to others. Educational office personnel are generally tuned into this form of communication.

For years women have been thought to have a certain way of translating feelings: women's intuition. Lately, behavioral scientists have analyzed just what this intuition is. It is the ability to sense the feelings of the individual who is speaking or, perhaps, not speaking.

Because women are often raised and socialized to be in the helping professions, and to be wives and mothers, many of them have developed this ability to sense an individual's feelings. The educational office employee (almost 98 percent in the field are women) brings that skill to the job without even knowing it. However, this skill is not innate or inborn but learned. Many managerial training programs are incorporating "intuition" into the curriculum.

Feelings, the intangible of communication, play an enormous role in the process.

SYMBOLS

Before an individual speaks to you with words, and before you have sorted out and analyzed the body language and nonverbal clues, he or she has sent you a powerful message about beliefs, values, lifestyle, affluence, and possibly even politics.

Symbolic communication is one of the most elusive, because it is seldom seen as a mode of communication. But communicate it does.

For example, you work in a conservative small town and the high school has about 300 students. One day, as you are working at the counter, a mother walks in to register her teenage son. She is wearing a very expensive suit, and the scent of her exotic perfume seems to permeate the room. The son is dressed in tattered jeans. His hair is long and unkempt, and he has a beard and mustache. In addition, he has an earring in one ear. Before that mother and student even open their mouths, you have evaluated the picture and possibly made some judgment about them, their lifestyle, their economic status, and their values.

Perhaps the picture is overstated. But this type of symbolic communication goes on in every setting we enter. It is crucial for the educational office staff to be aware of this.

If the way these people are dressed changes the way the parent and child are treated, the staff members are being influenced by their own attitudes and feelings. These feelings must be explored and sorted out. Unless people are aware of the feelings that symbolic communication can engender in them, they can easily believe they are supportive, democratic communicators, when in reality they are easily influenced by the symbolic communication of others.

THE PROCESS

We've discussed the ways people communicate—words, nonverbal communication, emotions, symbols. Now let's take a look at the actual transaction, and the ways the transaction can be improved.

In the figure shown, we have a sender of a communication and a receiver. The message is sent and received. Once it is received, the roles are reversed and the receiver becomes the communicator as he or she responds to the original message. Sounds simple, doesn't it? But take a look at what happens in the process.

Every communication passes through a filter, a frame of reference, of the individual's past experiences. Thus, words often mean different things to different people (i.e. dog), resulting in the chance for misinterpretation.

Couple this problem with the poor listening habits most people have. Seldom do people listen to a communication in its entirety. More often, they are preparing a response or rebuttal to the message, thus missing out on parts of the message. However, it is not surprising that people are poor listeners—they do so at 25 percent efficiency. People speak at 125 words a minute; yet one can understand at three to four times that rate. Therefore, a listener is faced with three options:

Frame of reference

1. actively listen
2. think of other things (rebuttal, response)
3. let thoughts wander.

Furthermore, when analyzing face-to-face communication, we find another element: only 10 percent of our meaning is transmitted by words. Thirty to 40 percent of meaning is extracted from the way words are used (intonation, sentence structure, etc.). The balance, possibly over 50 percent, is conveyed nonverbally (eyes, body language, gestures, posture, etc.).

Yet, communication is still more. In addition to transmitting information when they speak, people also send out powerful but silent messages of how they feel about themselves. An individual's self-concept comes through loud and clear, either through the choice of words, the way words are used, or nonverbal clues. A child who lacks self-confidence is not difficult to spot.

In addition, people's willingness or reluctance to self-disclose provides the astute communicator with invaluable information. This can aid the office staff in providing services.

A final aspect of communication is the way people deal with their anger. Often the person entering the school office is angry, perhaps not with the school office staff, but with someone else. How that person handles anger gives the office staff valuable insight into how to help the individual without damaging the individual's sense of dignity and self-esteem.

TECHNIQUES

Given that communication is complex, what special techniques can the office staff use to enhance the process? The techniques cited below may enable the educational office employee to improve or enhance transactions:

Become sensitive to the unspoken messages people convey. Body language, glances, posture, voice level, and gestures often mirror hidden messages which individuals are reluctant to put into words.

Give instructions (whether to students, support staff, teachers, parents, or even administrative staff) in segments so that the receiver has an opportunity to fully understand the instructions and ask for clarification, if necessary.

Ask for clarification when the message you receive is not clear. Through this process you can determine whether you fully understand what has been said to you. Conversely, encourage others to feel comfortable in questioning your instructions.

Encourage individuals to paraphrase the communication, putting it in their own words. Through this process the communicator realizes how the words and instructions were interpreted. Since words often have different meanings to different people, this technique will highlight what the receiver believes the words mean.

Finally, summarize what both people in the communication have said. Through summarization, each person focuses on what really transpired and what the future actions will be. This one step can avoid the typical response heard so often, "But I didn't know this was what we agreed to."

Thus far we have enumerated the concepts gathered under the seemingly innocent title of "communication." The balance of this chapter will be devoted to on-the-job application. Concepts, techniques, and application will be discussed through the use of brief scenarios. Although each scene is written and developed with a different group in mind, the application and strategies are not limited to that particular segment of the school public. Each scene and each application can just as easily be used in conjunction with any other group of individuals dealing with the educational office.

COMMUNICATING WITH ADMINISTRATIVE STAFF

Anyone who has been around school or administrative offices for any period of time knows that they all share a common characteristic—the pace is rapid. Communication takes place to get the job done; however, because of the pace, the quality of the transaction may leave something to be desired. Communications may be efficient in terms of time, but inefficient because of the interpersonal difficulties created. Later, these take enormous amounts of time to rectify.

In this segment we will explore interpersonal communications in the office, focusing primarily on the interplay between office staff and administrators. Let's look at a fairly typical setting.

SCENE

The setting is a crowded office. The phones are ringing, students are milling in the hall, and people are waiting at the counter to be served. The noise level is high.

The administrator emerges from her office and hands the secretary several pages of statistical typing. The superintendent is visiting and needs the work done immediately.

The secretary smiles, accepts the work, reaches for a ringing telephone, and motions to the clerk to come to the desk. After replacing the phone on the cradle, the secretary hands the typing to the clerk and states that the typing is needed immediately.

The clerk begins to argue that there is a stack of typing to be done —all of which has top priority—but is quickly silenced by a pleading look from the secretary. The clerk returns to the typewriter, rolls the paper into the machine, and begins to type, striking each key with a little more pressure than is required by an electric typewriter.

An hour later, the work is completed. As the superintendent gets ready to leave with the typed work, he stops to thank the secretary. The administrator comments that they are always happy to serve. The secretary comments that this is, indeed, an efficient office, and the clerk just smiles weakly. The secretary and clerk glance at each other knowingly.

The Task   Analyze the scene. What were the dynamics of the communication? Look at the process from the vantage point of each individual involved.

Communication Inhibitor	Result
Noisy office	Reduced efficiency, increased tension and stress
Status of administrator and superintendent	Reluctance of principal to admit staff was busy
Lack of self-disclosure by secretary	Reluctance of secretary to refuse work or ask principal to ask superintendent to wait
Lessening of self-esteem of secretary	Acceptance of work from principal, even though busy, and delegation of work to clerk. Both secretary and clerk know that the work should not have been accepted. Secretary suffers loss of esteem in own perception as well as in perception of clerk, because both recognized that the work should have been refused, but both felt powerless to do the refusing.
Refusal of clerk to deal with own anger	Anger manifested through clerk's striking keys harder than necessary. Anger is suppressed and not shared.
Collusion of "We're all one big happy family, eager to serve."	The principal pretends they are delighted to do the extra work; the secretary comments on the efficiency of the office; and the clerk smiles weakly. Everyone plays the game of "It's okay."

Results   Everyone in the scene is a loser. The superintendent can continue to drop in with his work. He thinks he is welcome and that the staff does not mind the extra work. Even if he knows the work is an extra burden, he can continue to pretend it is not, as long as staff continues to accept it and does not communicate with him.

The principal has let the office staff down. She was intimidated by the status of the superintendent and was reluctant to refuse a request, even though it was unreasonable. But the principal has thus suffered a loss of esteem in the eyes of the office staff. The additional work load was unfair, and everyone knew it.

The secretary suffers in the transaction, too. Although the work assignment was accepted by the secretary, the actual job was done by the clerk, who would not or could not refuse. Communication was silenced by virtue of their positions—again, status was an effective communication inhibitor.

One further communication barrier emerged—all agreed that they were pleased at the transaction; all agreed not to be open, not to share, not to be trusting of one another.

We are well aware that the reader may argue that there was no choice. The superintendent is the superintendent, and no one with any intelligence would refuse the work. No doubt there is validity in the argument. However, the purpose of presenting the scene was not to say how it should have been handled, but to enumerate the many communication inhibitors occurring in a school or administrative office with a status system. Perhaps the reader cannot change the system. But perhaps, just perhaps, one can.

No chapter on communication in the educational setting would be complete if the exquisitely subtle dynamics of status between certified and support staff were not acknowledged. It is a little written about, but much talked about fact. Educational office employees are aware of status, but choose not to discuss it. The purpose of mentioning it in this chapter is to acknowledge that this is a choice—with a price. The tragedy is that not only does the office staff pay the price, but everyone involved in education, from student to superintendent, does too. Writing about status and acknowledging it may be the first step in alleviating its effects on communication.

COMMUNICATING WITH OFFICE STAFF

> "Bob, would you do me a favor? I need this report typed as soon as possible. Double-space it. Start a new paragraph at each new thought. Then run me ten copies. Any questions? No? Great!"

Sound familiar? Anyone who has worked in a school or administrative office knows that this scenario is not exaggerated. The pressure of time, the volume of noise, and the sense of closeness and lack of privacy created by many people milling about—all make it extremely difficult to practice clear communication and effective listening. Unfortunately, the scene depicted, duplicated in countless offices, is filled with opportunities for miscommunication. Let us run the scene again and take a look at a few of them.

The supervisor began by asking Bob to do a favor. The question that must be posed is whether Bob has an option to refuse. If the implication is that he cannot refuse, then it is not a question, is it? It is what is commonly known as a pseudo question, a statement veiled as a question. Other pseudo questions include:

"Would you mind doing this for me?" If the person cannot refuse, then it is not a question, but a command, "Do this for me."

"Would you like to have more help to complete the project?" Translate this as, "I think you need help."

"Bob, you really want me to do that, right?" Could Bob say no? The question manipulates the listener into saying what the communicator wants.

"This office really has to become more efficient. Would you agree to that?" This traps the respondent. If the response is no, then the implication is that the office cannot become more efficient. If the response is yes, then obviously the person is agreeing that in the past it has been inefficient. The options lead equally to no-win situations.

Back to our first scenario.

The communicator gave Bob a series of instructions, but did not pause inbetween. At the end of the instructions, Bob is asked if he has any questions. However, the communicator does not wait for an answer, but co-opts Bob further by answering for him and then leaving.

How should instructions be given?

First of all, each segment should be given separately. At the end of each instruction, the listener should be given the opportunity to repeat the instruction so that it can be determined if the communicator said it correctly and if the listener heard every aspect. If the instructions are brief, the communicator can ask the listener to summarize at the end to determine if the transaction was clear.

Time also plays a factor. If Bob senses that his supervisor is busy, he may feel that it is risky to stop and ask for clarification. Here the status of the communicator hinders the communication process; therefore, it is his or her responsibility to diminish that factor by making sure that Bob feels comfortable in seeking clarification, additional information, or confirmation that he understood the communication.

Briefly stated, there should be an opportunity, when training or giving instructions, for the individual to clarify what is heard, repeat the information, and summarize to make sure both agree on what is to be done. Additionally, there should be abundant opportunity for the secretary/communicator to come back and check to see whether the work is progressing properly.

Now, project what the possible culmination of this scenario will be.

As it stands, Bob has a good chance of doing the work incorrectly. As a result, his supervisor may feel that he is not capable. In addition, if there is a deadline, his supervisor may feel let down by Bob.

Bob, on the other hand, will have put in the same effort whether the job is done correctly or not. Therefore, Bob will most likely feel resentful because his supervisor did not make the instructions clear.

There is an old saying, "We never have time to do a thing right, but there is always time to do it over." Perhaps that adage got started because people do not take the time to give clear, concise, and understandable instructions. And the listener does not have the opportunity to clarify, paraphrase, and summarize what is heard.

Let's run some other scenes. Only this time you supply the process. Any suggestions?

COMMUNICATING WITH THE COMMUNITY

SCENE I

Mrs. Jones parks her expensive car in front of the school. Even before she enters the office, the scent of her expensive perfume precedes her, gently enveloping the office. Mrs. Jones is impeccably dressed. She walks deliberately and briskly up to the counter, smiles, and in a firm voice asks to see the administrator. You rise and move up to the counter.

SCENE II

The school is situated in a changing area. A middle-class group is being replaced by a lower socioeconomic population. As a result of increased federal aid, the responsibilities in the office have increased and the number of reports has multiplied.

At the end of an especially hectic day, a parent enters the office with her child in tow. The parent seems hesitant and stands at the counter waiting to be served. The youngster waits rather impatiently. You look up and realize that another family has moved into the area and the child must be enrolled.

As a school secretary, you are asked to survey the situation and determine what steps to take. Yet, before considering the problem of what to do, stop and consider the communication that is going on. Ask yourself the following questions:

1. How are the parents communicating to the office staff?
2. What subtle methods of communication are being used?
3. How is the office staff going to respond? What messages that may not even be noticed influence the school secretary?
4. Will the steps taken differ in each scene? How do they differ? Why do they differ?

At first glance, these brief case studies may seem contrived. The mental pictures conjured up are distinctly different, yet they are similar. Admittedly the point is that the reader brings past experiences and values to the situation. In working with the public and communicating with them, we are influenced by all of our experiences, many of which we are unaware.

Let's take each scenario and analyze the communication going on, verbal, nonverbal, and symbolic.

In Scene I, Mrs. Jones has communicated to you in many ways. The car she drives indicates a certain economic status—or at least that she wishes to be measured by that standard. Obviously, an expensive car can mean status in a variety of ways. Most important, it is being translated by the school secretary in a particular way. The secretary may be impressed by the car, or may consider it a negative status symbol (ostentatious). Whatever is believed, the car has communicated something to the secretary and has become part of the communication process.

Scent or smell is also a strong communicator. In this case, the perfume has been identified as an expensive brand, projecting a particular image and influencing the secretary in a positive or negative way.

The parent's manner of dress is significant. People convey their self-concept by the way they dress. In addition, they also convey what they value in life. For example, someone who dresses in casual clothes may be saying something about his or her values in life. (Note the word "may" because clothing alone does not give us the total message.) Even if we "read" clothing incorrectly, we do "read" it as a communicator.

Next walk is important to note. Body language and gestures are another means by which people communicate. Mrs. Jones is deliberate in manner, suggesting purposefulness and the way she wishes to be seen and responded to. She smiles, thus denoting friendliness. Yet, her voice is firm as she requests to see the administrator.

The school secretary rises to respond to Mrs. Jones. Considering the mental picture and the communication process, it is not difficult to project what the treatment will be. However, Mrs. Jones may be treated other than expected. Possibly the office staff member finds it ostentatious to drive a new car. Or possibly, considering the energy crisis, she sees it as unpatriotic to drive that brand of car.

Additionally, Mrs. Jones comes in often. She is well known to the staff and has a tendency to demand rather than ask for help. The office staff feels she is a bit snobbish and intimidating. Here, the communication process may very well be clouded by a variety of feelings, most of them negative. Perhaps Mrs. Jones may not receive the treatment she was expecting.

In Scene II, the picture changes. We visualize someone who has not had an easy life. Her hesitant manner tells you she is not sure of herself. Perhaps she needs reassurance. The child seems restless. Will he turn out to be a discipline problem? The woman seems weary—another working mother who won't be around when the child becomes ill, perhaps a family that will generate more forms, more paperwork, more phone calls.

The mother walked in the door and the school secretary has received a variety of communications, although not a word was said. That, in itself, is significant. Reluctance to speak is often translated into messages which the receiver acts upon. Possibly, those signals are quite far from the truth.

To some people schools denote status. Based on past experiences with bureaucracies and individuals with a higher education, such a person might find the school formidable—a place to go when you have to, but a place that makes one feel less than important. Thus the parent, on entering the school office, may be dealing with many feelings. Sensitive school office personnel must be aware of these subtleties. Even the most unintentional gesture or frown can be translated into unacceptance, perhaps even rejection. All this without a word's being uttered.

In the communication process of the second scene, the body language, the symbolic message, even the feelings have transmitted strong messages before either one begins to speak. It is the role and the responsibility of the office personnel to make the message transmitted supportive, understanding, and nonjudgmental. A heavy job for generally overworked people—yet it is probably the most important job of the day.

COMMUNICATING WITH STUDENTS

> "What you are thunders so loud, I can't
> hear a word that you say!"

SCENE

John enters the office. He seems troubled and hesitates, clears his throat, and says haltingly, "Mrs. Riley?"

Mrs. Riley, who has been working on a report that is past due, raises her head, frowns, and in a stern voice replies, "Yes, John, can I help you?"

John begins to reply, mutters, "Never mind, I'll come back," and turns and leaves the office.

The scene is common enough, perhaps even the response is too. What were the communication processes going on?

When John entered the office, it was apparent that Mrs. Riley was busy. Through Mrs. Riley's body language of being preoccupied and not looking up, she sent the message as clearly as if she had said, "Don't bother me." He, in turn, also sent out a loud message by the way he entered the office haltingly, cleared his throat, and seemed reluctant to speak. Mrs. Riley then continued the process by the manner in which she raised her head, frowned, modulated her voice, and moved her body. In fact, although the words asked John what he wanted, her impatience was shown in the tone of her voice.

Instead of using the scene to highlight a better method of communicating, let's look at the unspoken messages that were transmitted. The words said one thing, but the feelings said another.

John's demeanor when he entered the office said a great deal about his self-esteem. He appeared unsure of himself, reluctant to intrude, not quite sure he belonged there. His message about himself, conveyed without uttering a word, indicated that he was uncertain—obviously not in control of the situation, and possibly a little apprehensive about being there.

In addition, he was reluctant to reveal why he entered the office in the first place. Unwillingness to disclose is not surprising in this situation. In order for there to be openness, there must be trust. Openness and self-disclosure are usually found to be in direct relationship to how comfortable a person feels. John was uncertain upon entering the office, and evidently the way he was treated gave him no reason to feel more comfortable.

Now look at the message transmitted by the secretary. It was apparent that she had a heavy work load. She was engrossed in the task. Upon raising her head, she frowned, suggesting displeasure. Whether she intended it or not is immaterial. The behavior she believed she transmitted was not known by John; what he responded to was his interpretation of her behavior. Obviously there may be miscommunication right there, with each person following assumptions that they do not check out. John responded to what he saw and translated it accordingly. Mrs. Riley's frown only confirmed what he already believed. Mrs. Riley's words were appropriate, but were offset by the tone which implied busy, hurry, deadlines, and impatience.

In summation, a transaction that may have taken less than half a minute is replete with messages: self-image, self-disclosure, impatience, body language, intonation, incongruency (nice words, negative intonation), and others.

We set the scene with a message in mind.

We all know the pressures on the school office staff. To ignore this fact of life is to do a great injustice and disservice to school staff members. Yet students are defenseless. They are dependent on the services of the office staff. Therefore, educational office personnel must be on guard and be cognizant of the subtleties of the communication process. The Johns of the scenario are alive and present in every school in the land. In determining how to help, we must all keep their vulnerability in mind. Remember: "What you are thunders so loud, I can't hear a word that you say!"

ASSERTIVE COMMUNICATION IN
THE SCHOOL OFFICE

Countless books enumerate the values of assertive communication. However, one often overlooked application is fundamental to the well-being of educational office employees everywhere—assertive communication in the office.

Through the use of assertive communication, conflicts can be settled, misunderstandings can be clarified, and the environment of the office can become one in which the dignity of each individual is protected without hurting others.

There are many definitions of assertiveness. For the purpose of this segment, we have defined assertive communication as:

> A means of communication whereby each person honestly expresses feelings, clearly understands the viewpoint and position of the other, and respects, not abridging nor denying, the rights or feelings of the others involved.

Assertiveness should be the base from which all effective people contacts in the office are made: contacts with teachers, administrators, parents, students, and other support personnel.

Before the application of assertive techniques is explored, an overall view of assertive training is needed, to help readers to gain perspective as well as to understand the complexity of the application.

Table 4-1 lists observable behaviors associated with three distinct communication styles: assertive, nonassertive, and aggressive. This table can serve as a checklist for the person who wishes to be an assertive communicator and needs help in distinguishing among the three styles. Learning the assertion techniques is the first step in becoming an assertive individual. Figure 4-1 illustrates the three levels of assertiveness.

Assertion techniques refer to the various responses used in assertive transactions. These include repeating, acknowledging, validating, and reiterating. Level II, assertive response style, refers to the actual behavioral

Table 4-1   Observable Behavior

Assertive

_____Displays confident body posture

_____Uses firm voice

_____Maintains appropriate voice level

_____Demonstrates personal control

_____Listens effectively in order to provide feedback

_____Acknowledges the other person's concerns

_____Affirms own position

_____Reaffirms if necessary

_____Uses "I" messages

Nonassertive

_____Uses poor eye contact

_____Displays defensive posture

_____Keeps voice level low

_____Speaks seldom

_____Backs up physically

_____Appears to be tense

_____Agrees too readily

_____Conveys weakness

_____Seems intimidated

Aggressive

_____Uses "you" messages

_____Keeps voice loud

_____Displays menacing body language

_____Uses psychological and verbal force

_____Practices inactive listening

_____Interrupts

_____Antagonizes

_____Argues

_____Does not acknowledge what the other person is saying

_____Uses killer phrases

_____Uses pseudo questions

differences distinguishing assertiveness from aggressiveness and nonassertiveness. The assertive lifestyle (level III) refers to the personal and social awareness of the individual—the ability to know the probable consequences of a particular behavior and to take responsibility for the consequences.

Now we will proceed to analyze each of these levels and look for applications in the educational office.

Assertive techniques (level I) provide a nuts and bolts approach to the everyday communications that regularly face the office staff. These techniques are quite simple:

Figure 4–1

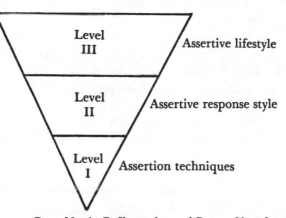

From Martin E. Shoemaker and Donna Olsen Satterfield, "Assertion Training: An Identity Crisis That's Coming On Strong," in Alberti, Robert E., Ph.D. (Editor), *Assertiveness: Innovations, Applications, Issues.* Copyright © 1977. Impact Publishers, Inc., San Luis Obispo, California. Reprinted by permission of the publisher.

Use "I" messages
Practice effective listening
Provide feedback
Validate concerns
Acknowledge that you understand the content of the message
Affirm your own position

As an example, consider the following scene.

SCENE

Teachers are supposed to allow two days lead time for work to be typed and reproduced. This rule was instituted because of problems that had occurred. Miss Brown often turns things in late, and exceptions have been made. This time the policy is to be firmly enforced and no exceptions will be made. Miss Brown is angry.

Miss Brown: You didn't do what I needed. I want you to type this right now.

Secretary: I sense you are really angry. I understand that you need the work for today. I wish I could help you, but the rule is two days' lead time for work to be reproduced. I am in the middle of this report and I can't do the work until tomorrow.

Miss Brown: I don't care about your problems—you don't care about mine. The two-day limit is unfair. Besides, you've always done it in the past. I need it today.

Secretary: I can understand that you feel disappointed. But you were at the faculty meeting when this was announced. I would really like to help you. In the past I was able to, but today the work load is too heavy. I'll have the work for you tomorrow.

Miss Brown: Can't you do me a favor? I promise I'll give you two days' notice next time. I need it now. You helped me the last time I got in a bind.

Secretary: I really sense your frustration. I know you would like it today. But if I did yours, I'd have to put aside Mr. Smith's work. I know you wouldn't want me to put your work aside for someone else. If I follow the rules, then everyone is treated fairly. I'm sorry, but I can't do your work until tomorrow.

Miss Brown: Well, please get it back to me in two days. And from now on I will follow the rules. I wouldn't want you to put my work aside for someone else either.

That is assertive communication in action. Of course it was staged. And of course we were looking for a happy ending. However, let's analyze the communication process to determine just what techniques were used.

The teacher was upset and blamed the secretary for not getting the work to her. In other words, she used "you" messages, assigning blame and guilt to the secretary.

The secretary acknowledged and validated the teacher's concern—effective listening. She used an "I" message, thereby telling the teacher what she sensed the problem was, in addition to what she felt the teacher was feeling. If the teacher felt she was not understood, she could clarify it at that time. By not using "you" messages, the secretary did not assign guilt. She just shared her perceptions.

The teacher continued to press and "attacked" by claiming that the secretary didn't care about her problems.

The secretary, if she had not been using "I" messages, could have responded in a hurt manner by saying that the teacher ("you") didn't care either. Instead, she affirmed the teacher's feelings again and explained the rules again. She may have been tempted to respond in a manner similar to the teacher's, but instead opted for the assertive mode and used another "I" message.

At this point the teacher proceeded to prey on the secretary's sympathy and point out past practices.

Again the secretary reaffirmed her understanding of the teacher's dilemma. She also involved the teacher by pointing out that if she did her work, she would have to put aside the work of a colleague. The secretary then restated the rules and why the rules were developed— everyone would be treated fairly.

Note that the secretary never took the attacks personally (sometimes a very difficult feat). She also continued to use "I" messages despite the "you" messages used by the teacher. Obviously this was a challenging situation.

One of the most difficult techniques in using assertiveness is that the people you are communicating with very often do not use the technique. Therefore, their statements can continue to be attacking and hurtful. Yet, if the individual can overcome the temptation to respond in a like manner, maintain composure, and use "I" messages, the rewards will be abundant.

This scene, as the reader is aware, was assertiveness at its best. Often, in actual practice, the scene is far more complex and the characters do not give in as readily. However, this does not diminish the effectiveness of assertive communication. It merely demonstrates how much the technique is needed as a basic tool of all educational office personnel.

If, despite angry people, unfair challenges, and difficult situations, the school secretary can keep cool, then everyone comes out a winner.

Although the treatment of assertiveness in this handbook is brief, the reader is encouraged to pursue the subject in the many books available, or in assertiveness classes. A list of books on the subject is included in the bibliography at the end of the chapter.

SUMMARY

In any enterprise where people are involved, communication skills are needed to convey messages. In education, be it in schools or administrative offices, communication takes on even greater significance because the product is essentially a service and the recipients of the service are impressionable students.

Therefore school secretaries and office employees need sophisticated communication skills. They must be aware of how communication transcends the fundamentals of talking and listening. They must understand that communication can be transmitted by words, nonverbal messages, emotions, and symbols.

In addition, there must be sensitivity to the various groups with whom they communicate and recognition of the specific techniques needed to work with such groups. These groups include administrators, teachers, other office staff members, parents, and community groups, as well as students.

Further, office staff members should be skillful in assertive techniques so they can proficiently deal with situations that could cause problems—and handle them in such a way that the other person feels his/her needs are being met.

By keeping in mind that communication includes words, listening, self-esteem, self-disclosure, and angry feelings, educational office employees can facilitate the smooth running of the office.

PROBLEMS

Problem 1

Plan a meeting with the clerical staff. Topics for the agenda could be:

1. The influence of symbolic communication.
2. Ways to implement assertive techniques when dealing with unreasonable people.
3. Methods of improving communication among the offices.

Either invite administrative staff to participate or share the results of the meeting with them.

Problem 2

Develop a checklist for the people in your office. The list should consist of typical ways people communicate and the typical communication problems that occur.

Share the list with the clerical and administrative staffs, and ask for their suggestions. Make each person aware of the list, and plan a training program for the new clerical members and student workers.

Problem 3

Practice your method of greeting people at the counter in front of a mirror. Be especially aware of the way you smile, your gestures, and the way you carry your body. Does the image convey what you want it to? What can you do to improve the way you are seen by people?

After trying this technique at home, suggest that office staff members practice observing each other. This way everyone is aware of the symbolic communications sent out and the influence they have on the people who enter the office.

Problem 4

Refer to the examples of communication problems cited in the chapter. Discuss with other office staff members how each would handle the situation. Then role play and practice proper techniques. Help each person become aware of the subtleties of communication and ways in which each can improve his or her methods.

Bibliography

Alberti, Robert E., ed. *Assertiveness: Innovations, Applications, and Issues*. San Luis Obispo, Calif.: Impact Publishers, 1977.

Alberti, Robert E., and Emmons, Michael L. *Your Perfect Right,* 2nd ed. San Luis Obispo, Calif.: Impact Publishers, 1974.

Chartier, Myron R. "Five Components Contributing to Effective Interpersonal Communication," in *The 1974 Annual Handbook for Group Facilitators*. LaJolla, Calif.: University Associates, 1974.

Pfeiffer, J. William. "Conditions Which Hinder Effective Communication," in *The 1973 Annual Handbook for Group Facilitators*. LaJolla, Calif.: University Associates, 1973.

Pfeiffer, J. William, and Jones, John E. "Don't You Think That . . . ? An Experiential Lecture on Indirect and Direct Communication" in *The 1974 Annual Handbook for Group Facilitators*. LaJolla, Calif.: University Associates, 1974.

Pfeiffer, J. William, and Jones, John E. "Openness, Collusion and Feedback," in *The 1972 Annual Handbook for Group Facilitators*. LaJolla, Calif.: University Associates, 1972.

Schmuck, Richard A., et al. *Second Handbook of Organization Development in Schools*. Palo Alto, Calif.: Mayfield Publishing Company, 1977.

Chapter 5

Supervising, Training, and Evaluating the Office Staff

The constantly changing role of the educational office supervisor creates the need for a method of supervising that is responsive to the dynamics of change. Increasingly, new supervisory techniques focus on the needs of subordinates. Quests to improve the quality of working life point out the uniqueness of the individual. Yet organization development considers the individual employee as but part of the total picture—in this case, the educational system. The techniques and concepts in this chapter should aid the educational office supervisor as he or she assumes more and more complex responsibilities.

Supervising, training, evaluating—background in the sophisticated theories of these three disciplines has become indispensable to the educational office manager. Supervising consists of more than telling people what to do. Training means more than giving instructions and hoping that the employee will do the job correctly. And evaluating is a tool for supervisors to motivate, guide, and help employees.

The true and false quiz in Figure 5 1 (p. 72) is provided to help readers explore their perceptions of the supervisory role. Please take that quiz before you proceed any further.

Your responses to the opening true and false quiz may have provoked a great deal of thought about the qualities you believe are required of an effective educational office supervisor. Many variables influenced your choice of answers. As with many true and false quizzes, you believed you needed more information. The question did not state enough. Your answer would depend on the situation.

If these are some of the thoughts that crossed your mind, then our goal has been achieved. Supervision does not have absolutes. For every statement advanced, there are many arguments against it. For every example given, exceptions to the rule can be cited. Supervision techniques in school offices reflect many variables.

Figure 5–1   Supervision

	T	F
1. Office supervisors should treat each member of the clerical staff in the same manner.	___	___
2. Rules must be followed so that people know where they stand.	___	___
3. The training of the office staff is the responsibility of the office supervisor.	___	___
4. The evaluation of employees is solely the responsibility of the administrator.	___	___
5. People who have been on the job many years should be given the same type of evaluation as someone who has been on the job for two years.	___	___
6. In every office, at least two people should know how to perform each function.	___	___
7. Office staff should be permitted to evaluate the office supervisor.	___	___
8. Some employees serve best when given specific tasks and a great deal of supervision.	___	___
9. Office supervisors should supervise in terms of the subordinates' needs, not their own.	___	___
10. An efficient educational office supervisor is involved in every aspect of the school office.	___	___

One variable is the attitude of the administrator. We recognize that the amount of supervision exercised by the office supervisor is greatly influenced by the style of the administrator in charge.

Another is the differences in people being supervised. We often read articles and hear educators comment on how the student of today is different from his or her counterpart of the past. Students today are more worldly because of television, more independent because so many mothers work, and more discerning because they evaluate instead of just accept. This quality of independence is not occurring just in the classrooms. Obviously, many of the students of today are becoming the educational office employees of today and tomorrow. This changing attitude of the office employee has received attention in industry as well as in education. Supervisory techniques of yesterday may not be effective on the office employee of today.

Recognizing the existence of these and other variables, we formulated this chapter to present a general overview of the latest supervision techniques. The one underlying assumption is that the office supervisor can be an essential and positive element in the efficient management of the office.

This chapter will approach supervision in terms of the needs of two groups: office supervisors, who need effective supervisory techniques, and school office staff, who will be more effective when supervisory methods take into consideration their needs as employees and people. We have used descriptors such as secretary, office supervisor, and school office manager interchangeably, since the person responsible for running the office may be called by many names.

SITUATIONAL LEADERSHIP— THE EFFECTIVE SUPERVISOR

We view the supervisor as

a teacher

a counselor

a confidant

a taskmaster

a friend

a supporter

Which descriptor applies will depend on the situation. The supervisor thus has the additional responsibility of discerning which quality would be most effective at a given time.

In addition to the qualities listed, effective supervision implies the ability to provide a working environment with the following components:

1. task
2. relationship

It is up to the supervisor to determine how much of each is required to achieve results.

Translating this into the school office environment, task refers to the work to be done. An effective supervisor must be able to train people to do the task or have training available through another source. Relationship refers to the environment in which people work. The proper amount of talking, support, and friendliness creates a climate that helps people work to their fullest potential. An effective supervisor must be able to maintain the work group so that staff meets deadlines, without unleashing tempers or sacrificing quality.

Effective supervision suggests that the office manager has a sixth sense, the ability to mix appropriate measures of task and relationship in order to reach the goals of the office. That sixth sense is one that can be developed. Implicit in deciding how much of each to use is determining the needs of the subordinates.

For example, the supervisor who feels that the office is one happy family and that happy people will work may provide a great deal of "relationship" and very little "task." However, employees may then view work as a party where everyone gets along but very little is accomplished.

At the other extreme is the supervisor who feels that people must keep their attentions focused on the job. There is no joking in this type of office; people are there only to work. Laughter is discouraged, talking is prohibited, and people must be watched.

Finally, we come to the effective supervisor, the one who knows that people work best with the right combination of task and relationship. Moreover, the effective supervisor also knows people need differing amounts of task and relationship. One formula does not fit all: the situation and the people involved determine how much of each component is needed. This theory, developed by Hersey and Blanchard,[1] is called situational leadership. Let's examine the dynamics of this concept and apply it to different situations.

SCENE I: THE NEW EMPLOYEE

Betty is a new clerk. This is her first job in a school. She is proficient in typing and office techniques.

Supervisory Style   Although Betty comes to the job with general office skills, she is a newcomer to the school office setting. Therefore, she requires a great deal of instruction in what her job entails. Although she may be interested in the people who are in the office, at this point Betty is far more interested in the technicalities of the job.

A capable office manager recognizes Betty's need for structure and support, makes sure she has instructions on how to do the job, is readily available if Betty has questions, and provides her with feedback on how she is doing.

Betty is introduced to other members of the staff, but generally concentrates on her new responsibilities. In other words, she is left alone

---

[1] Paul Hersey and Kenneth H. Blanchard, *Management of Organizational Behavior: Utilizing Human Resources,* 3rd ed. (Englewood Cliffs, N.J.: Prentice-Hall, 1977).

to learn the task—her new job—and, although people are around if she needs them, the relationship aspect of her job is kept to a minimum.

SCENE II: THE SIX-MONTH EMPLOYEE

Betty has been on the job for approximately six months. She is still in the process of learning her job. This is significant in education, where a complete cycle takes a year. For example, an office employee who begins a new job in July will not see the cycle repeat until the following July.

Supervisory Style　As Betty begins to be comfortable in her job and gains confidence in performing the tasks, she becomes more aware of the people around her. Friendships are formed and she begins to be a part of the social structure of the office. Although she needs a supervisory style that supplies the task support she needs, she now needs relationships with others, friendship, and support.

This is contrasted with her former needs, when a new employee, to learn the job and gain confidence. She also needed to have feedback from her supervisor on every aspect of the job. While this need may still exist, she also needs a friendly atmosphere, one in which people help and support each other.

As the reader can see, how much task and relationship should be provided by the supervisor depends on how much of each the subordinate needs, not on what style of supervision is most comfortable for the supervisor. Many supervisors experience difficulty in effectively supervising because their style reflects what they would like and what they believe the subordinates should have, rather than what the subordinates need. As we continue to explore the dynamics of situational leadership, the common thread binding all four styles will be the ability of the supervisor to discern and supply subordinates with the style most helpful to them, despite what the supervisor wants to do.

SCENE III: THE MORE EXPERIENCED EMPLOYEE

As Betty moves on in the continuum of proficiency in her job, her needs for supervision change.

Supervisory Style　Betty is now proficient in every aspect of her job. She has seen a full cycle, knows what to expect, and comes in and works with very little supervision. Although Betty continues to need the friendship and support of her supervisor, she has become an integral part of the social structure of the office. She continues to need to feel confident that her supervisor is there if needed, but verbal support and a feeling that she is part of the team become primary at this point. She participates in the decisions affecting her job and feels that her contribution is wanted and needed.

Betty maintains her work schedule, finishes assignments on time, and meets short- and long-term deadlines—obviously a self-motivated employee. It is at this point that many supervisors have difficulty. They accept the role of instructing the employee; they provide the relationship, friendship, and supportive atmosphere needed. However, when they should leave employees alone to work at their job, and no longer be involved in decisions affecting their subordinates, nor be consulted every time the employee faces a problem, supervisors often have the greatest difficulty.

Saying that delegating is important is easy, but actually delegating and permitting the employee to make decisions without input creates a dilemma for many office managers. Yet, it is from this fine art of delegating that supervisors will reap their greatest rewards. Essentially, it means the supervisor has trained the employee well; it also means the selection of the employee was good because the person is capable of fulfilling all the responsibilities of the job. The problem is that some supervisors feel it means they are no longer needed. Although this perception is a fallacy, it can profoundly influence the supervisor who believes it.

Many supervisors pride themselves on training subordinates to be independent, then demand that subordinates check with them on any unusual circumstance, instead of permitting the subordinate to use the judgment and training provided. Fear of not being needed has kept many supervisors tied to their jobs. Because the supervisors do not permit subordinates to really learn their jobs, when promotions are available administrators cannot promote the supervisors because there is no one around who knows their job and has had experience in doing it. Lack of meaningful delegation has kept many supervisors from moving ahead. In their desire to be needed, they have made themselves so necessary to the job that they cannot be spared for a new opportunity.

If supervisors apply the situational leadership concept, supervising only as much as is necessary, they will develop people who can move up to their own position when new opportunities open up.

SCENE IV: THE COMPLETELY TRAINED EMPLOYEE

At this stage, Betty is fully functioning, needs very little guidance or support from the supervisor, and can work on her own.

Supervisory Style   "Hands off" is the message for the supervisor. This employee will come to you if help is needed. In the meantime, permit the individual to do the best job that can be done. Assuming that the training program is good, and the environment provides the resources needed to do the job, this employee will do the job and do it well.

One crucial component of situational leadership is the acknowledgment that as situations change, so do the needs of employees. For example, a change would occur if, after Betty had been on the job several years and reached the point of being fully trained and completely independent, word processing were to be introduced into the school and all the methods of recording information were changed. At that point, Betty's supervisory needs would have changed. She would require a great deal of task and support. As a supervisor, you would need to be aware of this and provide the supervision style required.

A common complaint voiced by experienced secretaries is that because they do their jobs well, their administrators figure they can do anything and everything well. Therefore, even when there is a need for instruction, the administrators assume that their secretaries do not need it. Because of a reluctance to admit that they do not know, many secretaries muddle through and figure out new systems rather than asking for help.

If administrators supervised their secretaries using situational supervision, they would recognize that new policies and new procedures create a need for far more task and structure. Despite the fact that office employees have been on the job for many years and are outstanding in skills, new procedures create the need for different styles of supervision.

Conceptualizing situational supervision and putting it into practice may be difficult, but the rewards will make the effort worthwhile. Certainly the penalties of not using situational supervision are costly.

The employee who is never permitted to make decisions soon becomes dependent on the supervisor for every step and needs guidance even on the most menial task. The supervisor is trapped.

Another example is the supervisor who insists that everything be done one way, despite the fact that the employee has been on the job long enough to develop an equally good system. Every time the employee does it the supervisor's way, he or she is being forced to bend to the supervisor's will. The person who feels she or he has more to give will soon find an outlet for creativity in a better job. Then the supervisor will be faced with training another subordinate.

Situational supervision does not suggest that the office manager relinquish total responsibility. It merely suggests that effective supervision creates an atmosphere where people can become self-actualizing. With proper training and support, the employee can become a truly important member of the office team.

The application of this theory in the educational office setting requires one more component: the support and knowledge of the administrator. Since the perception of the administrator may be that an effective supervisor monitors and gives suggestions continually, supervisors face the dilemma of being labeled poor employees because they are not giving constant supervision to a subordinate who has mastered the job and is doing well. If an administrator measures effectiveness by activeness, then he or she could possibly evaluate the supervisor who uses situational leadership as incompetent or lazy. The dichotomy between what is effective supervision versus what is believed to be effective supervision is a problem that the office supervisor may have to discuss with the administrator.

Situational supervision involves using techniques appropriate to the task and relationship needs of subordinates. Figure 5-2 can help you analyze your supervisory style in terms of these factors.

Figure 5–2   Supervision Questionnaire

Is your supervision style sensitive to the needs of new employees?

Do you provide the task structure needed when an employee is new to the job?

When you delegate a responsibility, do you give the subordinate the resources to get the job done?

Do you insist that the clerk check with you on each step?

Do you feel that talking in a school office is not appropriate?

Do you feel threatened if people suggest different methods of doing a job to you?

Are you receptive to new ways of doing things, or do people have to do things your way?

Do you share your supervisory methods with your administrator?

In illustrating the concepts of situational leadership and supervision, we referred to the training process for new employees. In the next segment of this chapter, training techniques will be discussed.

TRAINING THE OFFICE STAFF

Traditionally, the training of office personnel has been left up to the secretary. Although districts are moving toward providing formal pre-service and in-service training, generally this continues to be the function of the office supervisor. In this section, we will focus on methods and procedures the supervisor can use to fulfill this important function.

One of the fundamentals in the training of new employees is a procedure manual. Contained in this manual are a description of all the responsibilities of the individual, a sample of the forms used to do the job (properly filled out), and a calendar of events. This manual is a critical element in the training of new employees. It provides continuity for new personnel and serves as an insurance policy when people are ill or leave unexpectedly. However, the procedure manual is only a guide. It is still up to the office supervisor to train personnel in office procedures.

The techniques illustrated in this section will not be specific in content. What they suggest are methods for training personnel in the way things are done in a particular office.

There is an old standard technique for training personnel:

You tell people what they need to learn and what you are going to teach them.

You show them what you want them to learn.

You watch them do it.

You give them feedback on how well they performed.

You give them the opportunity to try it on their own, making yourself available for questions and concerns if problems arise.

You give feedback on their progress.

We subscribe to this, but with one major addition: communication. New employees are dealing with many things:

meeting new people

adjusting to a new office

learning new procedures

impressing the supervisor

wondering and worrying about how they are doing.

Although a new employee may fully intend to concentrate when the supervisor is giving instructions on the methods to be used, there is a great chance that he or she may be too worried about any or all of the above to concentrate effectively.

In the chapter on communication, barriers were discussed. Preoccupation and status are two barriers that can create formidable problems for new employees. They are preoccupied worrying about their new job, how well they will perform, and whether they will like it. In addition, the supervisor has status and power over them and they do not wish to make mistakes. Therefore, when instructions are given and the new employee is asked whether there are any questions, the first response is usually, "No, I don't think so." After all, when trying to impress the supervisor, one is usually reluctant to admit lack of understanding. In addition, because the new employee may be somewhat preoccupied, good listening skills may not be used.

A supervisor skilled in training takes these factors into consideration and adds the critical element of effective communication to the process of training. By this we mean seeking questions, asking for clarification and paraphrasing, and, finally, using "enabling" behavior such as supportive body language to convey concern and interest to the trainee.

Let's look at the components of training and add the communication links.

STEP 1

You tell people what they need to learn and what you are going to show them. Communication link: After you enumerate the responsibilities (with the use of the procedure manual), you ask the employee if there are any questions about what is to be learned. By asking questions in a supportive manner, the supervisor makes the employee feel comfortable and unafraid to make mistakes in repeating information. A word about "dumb" questions: often trainees believe questions to be "dumb" because they feel they should have retained the information the first time it was given. It is up to the supervisor to set the climate by stating that no question is dumb since it helps clarify, and that by asking questions the employee gives guidance to the supervisor on what sections to clarify.

STEP 2

You show them what you want them to learn. Communication link: If a picture is worth a thousand words, a demonstration is worth a million. It is while the supervisor is demonstrating the technique that the employee can ask why, how, and what, and really find out what the procedure is all about. This applies to learning technical information as well as learning how to answer the phone. Supervisors often take for granted that everyone knows the reason behind procedures. A new clerk does not have a knowledge base. As the supervisor demonstrates, the clerk has the opportunity to find out vital information.

STEP 3

You watch them do it. Communication link: As the trainee performs the job for the first time, you find out how much of the first two messages about the procedure have reached their mark. While watching you can correct the trainee's performance. This must be done tactfully and supportively, however, so the trainee does not feel sensitive to the criticism or too nervous to hear it.

STEP 4

You give feedback on how they have performed. Communication link: Perhaps the product is not up to par. It is up to the supervisor to criticize gently. If the employee sees that failing in performing does not mean failing as a person, he or she will be more receptive to criticism in the future.

STEP 5

You give them the opportunity to try it on their own, making yourself available for questions and concerns if problems arise. Communication link: The employee is working alone. But if halfway through the process help is needed, the employee must be able to come to you for it. Often it is at this time that the communication link breaks down. The trainee who thinks you are too busy to be interrupted will refrain from asking important questions. And if the job is done incorrectly, the person will resent your unavailability for questions. Clearly, the communication link is a critical element in this step.

STEP 6

You give feedback on progress. Communication link: Another important old adage is that you praise in public and criticize in private. The employee needs feedback on how well the job was done. Each step should be either supported or changed, and the communication link is necessary in order to correct or encourage. The employee may well be apprehensive at this moment of truth; giving this feedback in private will alleviate anxiety. In addition, knowing that no one else is around to listen, the employee can fully concentrate on what you have to say, without worrying about others overhearing the conversation. Maintaining the dignity and trust of the trainee is critical if the supervisor is to be successful in the endeavor of training.

The employee's first experience in being trained has enormous significance for the future. The method of treatment in this process sets the stage for what will be expected in the future. The supervisor who trains in a manner that ensures dignity and success for the subordinate will have an employee who is receptive to training and suggestions. As the supervisor and trainee work together in building the necessary skills, they are also developing the trust and openness needed to foster teamness.

Getting the employee involved in learning—through demonstrations, communications, and hands-on training—has been proven to be a most successful method. Adults learn best when they are doing. However, doing must be coupled with communication to make sure the task is being done right. Adding the communication link to the process is one way the supervisor can ensure that the trainee will have a successful experience.

Figure 5-3 is a checklist to help you evaluate the training you provide to office staff.

Figure 5–3 Training Questionnaire

Has the trainee been given a procedure manual relating the responsibilities of the job?

Is the employee encouraged to ask "dumb" questions?

Do you encourage the employee to stop you as you demonstrate a new process so that questions can be asked?

Do you make yourself available throughout the training process so that the trainee can verify if the procedure is being performed properly?

Do you give feedback in private so that the trainee is not embarrassed?

Do you take into consideration that a new employee may be anxious about the new position and therefore have trouble listening?

Do you retain your sense of humor and patience when the employee does work incorrectly?

Do you ask for a clarification of your instructions in order to determine if you gave them correctly?

EVALUATING THE
EDUCATIONAL OFFICE STAFF

More and more, as school administrators recognize the abilities of office supervisors, they are delegating the responsibility of evaluating subordinates to them. This delegation of responsibility acknowledges the supervisory role of the secretary. The purpose of this section is to aid the secretary in developing sound evaluating procedures designed to help staff members achieve maximum potential.

One of the most common reasons people have difficulty in carrying out the evaluation process is because they do not have a reliable scale with which to measure. Although in this chapter we do not get into the testing process, we do suggest that it is within the school office manager's control to set up a method for fair evaluation. This will enhance the quality of working life of the employee and improve the service to the students.

The first tool is the job description: a list of duties for the employee. A job description serves as an indicator of what a supervisor can expect and what the employee should be capable of performing. Generally it lists typical duties the person is expected to perform, minimum education and job experience needed to be eligible for the position, as well as specific knowledge, skills, and abilities applicants should possess. This list is a basic tool in the evaluation process.

Unfortunately, many school districts do not have formal job descriptions for every position. Thus, it may be necessary for the supervisor to develop a description for the position to be evaluated. This step must be handled in conjunction with the site administrator. Often, this process uncovers the fact that some of the duties being performed are not what the administrator had in mind. This phenomenon has also occurred in countless administrator-secretary team building workshops (see Chapter 2).

The job description, prepared by the personnel department or the administrator-supervisor team, is a base for evaluation. Using it, one can determine what commendations, recommendations, and criticisms should be directed to the employee. It also helps the employee know just what is expected. A common complaint voiced by subordinates is that they feel they have been treated unfairly in the evaluation process because they never fully understood just what was required of them.

However, the job description is not enough. Coupled with it must be an on-the-job training program. With this combination, the performance evaluation takes on meaning: the employee knows what is expected and has been provided the training to do the job.

Moreover, the evaluation process is not meant just for the new employee. It is a continuing process that can reinforce good habits and change those habits which are not productive. Therefore, we will explore the evaluation process in terms of three levels of employees: the new employee, the two-year employee, and the veteran (the one who may provide the greatest challenge to the office supervisor).

Although, theoretically, the purpose of evaluating employees is to give them feedback on how they are performing on the job, many other factors enter into the process. For a new employee, the evaluation provides information on how well tasks are being learned. For one with a few years' experience, the evaluation may consider possibilities for upward mobility and expanded job options. For the seasoned veteran, it may help keep the individual on task when the job becomes so routinized as to be boring. Whatever the situation, when properly handled the evaluation process can be a valuable tool for the office supervisor.

THE NEW EMPLOYEE

Initially the new employee should be given a list of duties and on-the-job training (a subject covered under training of office staff). After training has been completed, the evaluation process becomes helpful.

An evaluation form should reflect the duties that are to be evaluated. Since such a form is not always readily available, the secretary may have to develop one. The task need not be that difficult.

Let's use the position of clerk typist as an example. Generally there are three major areas that are being evaluated:

Technical skills (typing, use of office machines, etc.)
Interpersonal skills (communication, public relations, getting along with others, etc.)
Ability to learn new skills

Under each area, enumerate the specific skills needed for the position. Then next to each skill describe specifically how well the subordinate is meeting the criteria for effective performance.

To help you develop your own evaluation form, use job descriptions if available. If your district does not have them, work with the administrator to develop your own.

Observations and suggestions included in the evaluation should be stated in terms that reflect actions that are observable, measurable, and legal. One of the complaints most often made by subordinates is that an evaluation was vague. For instance, "The secretary said I have a poor attitude. I don't know what that means."

"Attitude" must be translated into observable behaviors for the evaluation to take on meaning. For example:

> "You were rude on the phone—you answered in an angry tone of voice. You didn't give the parent the information that was requested."
>
> "People wait a long time to be served at the counter."
>
> "Your typing has to be done twice because of errors."
>
> "The statistical report had five errors. This occurred two months in a row."
>
> "When answering the phone, you don't give the name of the office and your name, which is the procedure used in this location."

As you can see, the types of behavior cited are specific; the employee knows what is needed to improve the performance.

The corollary of this is that praise should also be specific. Stating that a person does a nice job, without stating what, in particular, is good performance, leaves the person without any guidance on what to continue doing. Vagueness is the enemy of effective employee evaluation. A new employee especially needs a great deal of structure. It is in the formative months, when one is learning the tasks and routines of the office, that evaluation is most important. Hoping that the message will get across by inference is unfair—both to the supervisor and to the employee.

Yet the process need not be unkind. In essence, an evaluation can say some very positive things:

> "I believe you are doing certain duties well. I also believe that there are areas in which you can improve. Therefore, I am bringing these matters to your attention because I believe you are capable of change and improvement."

When a supervisor resists evaluating an employee because "It won't do any good," that individual has judged the subordinate incapable of change and improvement. When a supervisor makes no effort to correct an employee, he or she guarantees that the individual will continue to do less than an adequate job. What a heavy penalty for the employee, the district, and the supervisor.

Let's return to our new employee.

With the job description and the observations of measurable behavior in hand, the supervisor meets with the new employee. Prior to this meeting, the employee should have the opportunity to do a self-evaluation based on the same criteria the supervisor is using. By giving the employee the opportunity to evaluate work performance, the supervisor will gain insight into the employee's perception of the job, and the effectiveness of the on-the-job training. The self-evaluation may open the supervisor's eyes to problems only the subordinate could see.

The room setting for evaluation plays a significant role in the success of the process. The employee may feel anxious—after all, this is the moment of truth. Therefore, the setting should be relaxed and free of interruptions.

The "positive sandwich" approach, although usually applied to letter writing, is an extremely effective technique in evaluation: praise the areas that are performed well, follow with constructive criticisms and suggestions for areas to be improved, and end with praise and a feeling of optimism that the employee can bring the performance up to what it should be. If the supervisor opens with positive comments, the employee will be relaxed and more responsive to suggestions. Ending the evaluation on a positive note makes sense, too. Sandwiched inbetween are the specifics, which include one critical element. If you name areas where the employee is expected to improve and work with the employee to develop a plan for change, then the last step is to enumerate exactly how it will happen, how you will know when it has occurred, and by when it should have happened. The best evaluation interview becomes meaningless if both parties have not agreed to a timeline of when certain events will happen. If this does not occur, both parties probably are destined to meet again to discuss the same issues. History does repeat itself.

THE TWO-YEAR EMPLOYEE

The evaluation process may serve a dual purpose for the two-year employee. Presumably the individual has developed the skills and abilities to do the job. Therefore, although the evaluation process serves to reinforce and give correction, it also fills other needs of the employee. After several years on the job, the subordinate may be looking for expanded job options. The job may be becoming repetitious, possible boring. The excitement and challenge of learning a new job, meeting new people, and developing new skills may have waned. Here the evaluation process may be just the tool to inject new interest and enthusiasm into the job.

Career counseling and performance evaluation go hand in hand. Although a later chapter focuses on this subject in depth, we will touch upon it here in its relationship to evaluation.

The evaluation process is the ideal time for supervisors to discuss career plans with subordinates. When a new employee is hired, the district makes a substantial monetary investment in training. When administering the evaluation, the supervisor has the opportunity to point out career options within the district which may appeal to the employee. The supervisor can explore whether there is some way the present job can provide training required for the projected job. This technique of coupling career counseling and evaluation has several purposes:

1. It demonstrates that the supervisor cares about the subordinate's future.
2. It keeps the employee's interest at a high level, since job expansion prevents the current job from becoming stale and boring.
3. It may motivate new employees, who observe that the secretary really cares about subordinates. It gives them the incentive to work hard, so that when they have been on the job for a period of time and have mastered the skills, they too can look forward to the secretary's counseling them on career opportunities within the district.
4. It provides a very real incentive to the two-year employee to keep performance at a high level. Obviously, the supervisor will not and should not recommend people for advancement if they demonstrate poor work habits on the job they currently hold. Suggestions for improvement take on greater significance if the individual sees a reward system.

Suppose the employee's career goals lie outside the school district. This career counseling technique can still serve the district, for if the employee can readily see how today's experience can lead to tomorrow's job, whether inside or outside the district, he or she will bring new enthusiasm to the current position.

THE VETERAN EMPLOYEE

Perhaps the greatest challenge in the evaluation process may be evaluating the dedicated, loyal employee who has been on the job for many years, likes what he or she does, and has no intention of moving upward or outside. This person plans to work in the same position until retirement. Such employees place many a supervisor in a difficult position.

Since these employees have been on the job for years, they often feel secure that they know their jobs, and the supervisor's evaluation merely serves to reinforce their own evaluation of job performance. Generally this is true: knowledge is complete, and dedication to the job is unequaled—surely a supervisor's delight. Yet, there are cases where the employee has been on the job so long that he or she has forgotten the reasons behind many of the procedures. In fact, some aspects of the job may even have become unnecessary. The long-time employee often assumes that the job is being done well and is not receptive to hearing anything but an affirmation of good performance. It takes a brave supervisor to state otherwise. This is the evaluation process we wish to explore: how to tell the person who knows everything that the rules have changed and that performance must also change.

First of all, use the positive sandwich, but in moderation. If you start out with too many positive statements, the subordinate will agree with you and stop listening. Then comments about change will fall on deaf ears.

Secondly, before embarking on areas to improve, ask if the employee has any concerns with the position. The employee may be aware that things are not perfect, but may be reluctant to bring up the subject. Sometimes long-term employees assume that they should know all the answers, and thus it is difficult for them to ask for help. Opening the door for questions and concerns allows these employees to voice their problems. The evaluation process may provide the vehicle the veteran employee requires to address areas in need of exploration without losing face.

There is another dynamic here which cannot be ignored. Often the supervisor is younger than the subordinate. The subordinate may also have been on the job longer than the supervisor. The supervisor must be sensitive to this but affirm his or her own responsibility to evaluate. Tact, sensitivity, patience, and perseverance are the qualities that are needed.

As stated before, not telling employees how they can do better gives them no opportunity to improve—this guarantees that no improvement will take place. The long-term employee is entitled to an open mind on the part of the supervisor.

Finally, now that retirement ages are being extended, supervisors no longer have the luxury of waiting for ineffective employees to retire. It is up to the supervisor to help each employee realize his or her potential. The alternative is for the supervisor to live with the frustration of an employee who brings a diminished performance to the job. The supervisor must also live with the realization that in certain areas of supervision—namely, the evaluation process—it is the supervisor who may not be performing at an appropriate and effective level if evaluations do not help employees improve job performance. The techniques enumerated above should help the office supervisor to enhance or improve evaluating skills.

Before closing this segment on evaluation, we wish to suggest one additional method. The techniques that have been discussed so far have followed the tried and true approach of praise followed by suggestions and criticisms, followed by praise. However, a new problem-solving approach has been developed by Norman Maier. Described in detail in *The Appraisal Interview, Three Basic Approaches,* the problem-solving technique relies on the supervisor's interviewing the subordinate with a series of open-ended, nonthreatening questions which help the employee come to terms with areas that need improvement and options to improve the situation. It is nondirective and relies on the employee's being cooperative with and trusting of the supervisor.

Since the object is to stimulate growth and development, and not to criticize or censure, the problem-solving approach should come at a time when good relations exist between supervisor and subordinate. In addition, this process is not recommended at a time when the formal, written appraisal is being signed. Handled effectively, this approach encourages employees to acknowledge their weaknesses. Therefore, following such an interview with a written evaluation enumerating these areas may be perceived as unethical and certainly would destroy any measure of trust that existed.

In addition to proper timing, proper setting is important. It is essential that the setting of the problem solving be relaxed and interruption-free.

The supervisor opens the conversation with the acknowledgment that the meeting is to talk about how the employee perceives the job. The interview proceeds with open-ended questions based entirely on what the employee says. This technique often proves troublesome to the supervisor who wants to ask directing, probing questions and give specific suggestions for improvement. However, this is not the purpose of the problem-solving approach. This technique depends on the employee's acknowledging areas of weakness and suggesting methods to alleviate these areas.

Probably the greatest benefit of this method is that the employee suggests the methods to improve. This places the responsibility on the subordinate and not the supervisor. The weakness is that some employees may not be knowledgeable enough to solve their own problems or they may come up with solutions that the supervisor does not support. Despite this weakness, the method provides a sound alternative to the traditional method and should be explored.

Figure 5-4 will help you evaluate the techniques you are using in the evaluation of personnel.

Figure 5–4   Evaluation Questionnaire

Does the subordinate who is being rated know what is being evaluated?

Can you measure the performance being evaluated?

Do you give your subordinates the opportunity to evaluate themselves before they meet with you for the evaluation?

Have you developed a job description if none is available?

Have you checked with your personnel office to determine whether your requirements are consistent with local, state, and federal guidelines and laws?

Do you provide suggestions and criticisms that are measurable and observable?

The techniques of open-ended questions and effective listening which provide the foundation of the problem-solving approach are listed below:

Problem-Solving Approach to Performance Appraisal

1. *Open-ended questions*
   How has the job been for you?
   What's going well? What do you think contributed to that?
   What isn't going well? What do you think contributed to that?
   How would you like to change things?
   How can that be accomplished?
   What would you like to do?
   When do you think that will occur?
   How will we know when it does occur?
2. *Listening responses*
   Nodding
   Gesturing
   Smiling
   Using expressions such as "Hmm"
3. *Repeating responses*
   Repeating words that the person says to encourage and clarify
4. *Paraphrasing*
   Repeating what is heard in own words
5. *Checking perceptions*
   Clarifying feelings
   Validating own observations of person's feelings

6. *Silence*

Silence usually conveys the message that you're waiting and want more information.

It should not be used when the individual is upset. It will not relax him/her.

SUMMARY

Supervising, training, and evaluating—these three responsibilities are true measures of the effective office supervisor.

In supervising, the school secretary wears many hats: teacher, counselor, confidant, taskmaster, friend, and supporter. It is a supervisor's responsibility to analyze each situation and to decide which hat should be worn at that moment.

It is essential that the secretary establish a working situation with the correct combination of task (the work to be done) and relationship (the supportive environment in which people work). Each employee's needs should be analyzed so that the supervision is based on the needs of the subordinate, not the needs of the supervisor.

Each office supervisor has a responsibility to train subordinates, whether or not there is formal recognition of this task. In addition to using the standard techniques for training (telling them how to do it, showing them how to do it, watching them do it, and then giving feedback on how well they have done it), the effective supervisor adds another element: the communication link. This is necessary so that the employee can receive support, encouragement, and constant feedback on how well he/she is doing at each step. A new employee's training experience establishes the basis for the entire working relationship. Effective office supervisors do their best to make sure that the experience is both informative and pleasant.

In supervising, the office supervisor provides the environment the employee needs to do a good job. In training, she/he provides the knowledge the employee needs to do a good job. In evaluating, the supervisor provides the knowledge the employee needs to be on target—information on how well the working goals are being met. In order to evaluate well, one must have job descriptions so that the subordinate knows the measure against which he/she is being evaluated. If none are available, it often falls to the school office manager to provide them. When evaluating job performance, the supervisor must frame suggestions, criticisms, and praise in language that the employee can understand and apply. Therefore, recommendations should be measurable, observable, and achievable so that the employee can set goals to improve.

The educational office manager's role is changing. Nowhere is this more apparent than in the recognition office managers are gaining for their role as supervisor, trainer, and evaluator.

PROBLEMS

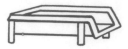

Problem 1

You have just joined a new office as office manager. The person before you was on the job for many years and was a respected member of the office staff. Clerical members consist of one younger clerk (who is new) and six mature women who have been on the job for many years.

A new directive has come from the central office, and several report procedures must be changed. This requires new procedures, new forms, and new deadlines. One of the mature employees has informed you that she is aware of the new procedures and has incorporatd them into her work.

After the first report is turned in, the central office calls to inform you that the report they received was prepared incorrectly. Your task is to bring this to the attention of the clerk. In recent weeks she has become more and more aloof and barely acknowledges your presence.

What steps do you take to correct the procedures she is using on the new report?

Describe the setting.

Who is present?

How will you handle it?

How will you ensure that the procedures are followed correctly in the future?

Problem 2

Dorothy is a secretary. She has one clerk who reports to her. There has been a succession of individuals in this position. Each has either quit or transferred to another office after a short period of time. When questioned about why they were leaving, all responded that there was too little to do. Yet Dorothy complains consistently about being overworked.

As the office supervisor over Dorothy, it is your responsibility to determine why there is such a high employee turnover and to work with Dorothy to alleviate the problem.

How do you handle it?

Problem 3

Jean has been a secretary for many years. She has had a staff of three clerks for a long time. Morale is high and work is generally handled promptly and efficiently.

However, a problem has developed recently. One of her experienced clerks left, and a young man, Karl, was hired. Jean introduced Karl to the other staff members, told him what to do, and requested that he ask if he had questions.

Karl is rather quiet and tries to do his work. Yet his performance is not good, and Jean believes she made a mistake in hiring a young man.

Karl acknowledges that people are friendly, but he maintains that no one is telling him what he should do.

Jean feels that she has shown Karl and that he is just slow.

Where do you believe the problem is?

What do you recommend that Jean do?

Should she fire Karl?

Problem 4

Mary Jones is the office supervisor. Because of an increased workload and expanded responsibilities, the decision has been made to add a clerk typist to the one-person staff.

1. Enumerate the steps Mary should take to train the new clerk.
2. Since there is no job description available, what should Mary do to develop one ?

Problem 5

Your supervisor has asked you to develop a procedure for evaluating personnel. In the past the process has simply involved sitting down and discussing the job. She wishes to move to a more formalized procedure, in which the rights of employees are safeguarded, yet goals are set for improvement.

She has asked you to meet with her in three weeks to discuss implementation of the new procedure.

What steps do you take?

What information do you need?

Whom do you need to involve?

Bibliography

Gordon, Thomas. *Leader Effectiveness Training.* New York: Wyden Books, 1977.

Hersey, Paul, and Blanchard, Kenneth H. *Management of Organizational Behavior: Utilizing Human Resources,* 3rd ed. Englewood Cliffs, N.J.: Prentice-Hall, 1977.

Maier, Norman R. *The Appraisal Interview, Three Basic Approaches.* LaJolla, Calif.: University Associates, 1976.

Owens, Robert G. *Organizational Behavior in Schools.* Englewood Cliffs, N.J.: Prentice-Hall, 1970.

Yoder, Dale, and Heneman, Herbert G., Jr., eds. *ASPA Handbook of Personnel and Industrial Relations: Training and Development.* Washington, D.C.: The Bureau of National Affairs, 1977.

Chapter 6

Conflict and Anger
in the School Office

You are about to embark on a challenging, innovative approach to conflict and anger. First, please respond to the statements in Figure 6-1. Save your responses to compare them with your answers at the end of the chapter.

Figure 6–1

1. Conflict in the school office is_____

_____

2. When faced with a conflict in the school office, I_____

_____

3. If administrators challenge the procedures I use, I_____

_____

4. When I am angry, I_____

_____

5. People who are angry should_____

_____

6. When someone makes an unreasonable request for work, I_____

_____

Although the subjects of conflict and anger are often merged, we will deal with each separately, since the techniques often vary.

CONFLICT IN THE OFFICE

Have you ever entered an office where everyone smiles and is gracious—yet you know something is drastically wrong? Despite the greetings and the nice words, your intuition tells you that what appears on the surface is not what really exists. There is a tenseness in the body language, the smiles, the actions. Something is there and you sense it.

That sense has not led you astray. What you have inadvertently stumbled into is a conflict in the office. Everyone knows that it happens; conflict occurs wherever people work together. Moreover, it is not always a negative matter. However, in school offices, because of the importance of a positive public relations image, staff members may take an unspoken vow not to permit the creature to emerge; they hope somehow it will disappear if left alone.

However, conflict seldom disappears—it merely submerges. When the conflict is not dealt with openly and productively, it may fester and take its toll in subtle but pervasive ways, such as absenteeism, reduced productivity, illness, employee turnover, veiled hostility, aggressive behavior cloaked in the garb of assertiveness. Or it may erupt in inappropriate ways—open hostility, arguments, fights.

Our purpose is to examine conflict from several angles, highlight the contribution it can make to a school or administrative office, and develop action plans to make conflict a productive and supportive mode of behavior.

Calling conflict productive or supportive may seem perplexing, since people tend to view conflict as a negative concept. It is difficult for many to accept conflict's positive qualities. But we believe that it is only when the myth of conflict is held up to scrutiny, and office staffs see how to use it productively, that visitors will cease to be faced with a scene similar to the one described at the beginning of this section. Conflict can and should become acceptable behavior, once people develop productive ways of dealing with it.

One of the major reasons conflict is not perceived as acceptable behavior is that generally, even when people do confront the issues of the conflict, nothing changes. This lack of action perpetuates the belief that conflict in any way, shape, or form is bad. However, conflict, when channeled and handled in a pro-active manner, can be the basis for negotiating improvements in the office climate. Our approach is that conflict may be the first concrete step toward growth, improvement, and openness. By openly facing the issue, by seeking the reasons behind a conflict, the office staff will have the opportunity to initiate productive changes in the way people behave toward one another.

Let's explore just what conflict is, how it emerges, and what the options are in dealing with it.

Avoidance or confrontation

Conflict, like beauty, is often in the eyes of the beholder. Just reflect on a situation that both you and another person view. A teacher comes in, speaks in a discourteous manner to you and the other clerk, and walks out. You continue working, while the other person seethes with tension. The other individual sees a conflict and you see nothing. In fact, your treatment of the situation might increase the other's anger. "Why aren't you bothered by it?" is the question. Generally, the answer is that in your view of the situation, a conflict did not exist.

Conflict is a very personal matter. When a conflict situation occurs, the viewer weighs the conflict, then decides how to respond to the situation. Basic to the process is the fact that the viewer must see the situation as some sort of challenge. Given that the situation does elicit a feeling of conflict in the viewer, there are still a variety of possible responses. According to Joan A. Stepsis, one might avoid the situation or confront it using either power or negotiation.

Some people opt to do nothing, avoiding a confrontation at any cost. While this technique may be productive under certain conditions, consistently avoiding issues often leads to a feeling of worthlessness.

For example, a secretary who consistently accepts last-minute work without protest may soon believe that he or she deserves this sort of treatment —in other words, a self-fulfilling prophecy. "If others treat me poorly by giving me work without any notification, if people think so little of me that they don't believe me worthy of consideration, then perhaps I am unworthy. Maybe they know something about me that I don't, and I really deserve to be treated this way."

If this sounds farfetched to you, search your memory for a person you know who consistently accepts poor treatment from others because of a firm belief that the others would not be willing to do anything to change their behavior. The effect of such individuals on the school office morale is incalculable and may be contagious. Other staff members may begin to accept this negative perception and view themselves as unworthy—thus lowering their own self-esteem. Or else the individual's sense of doom may result in others' avoiding his or her company or choosing not to work with him or her. This only serves to reinforce the negative feelings. As you can see, avoiding the situation generally does not lead to a productive solution to the problem.

Other people approach conflict with a defusing ploy—they joke or try to change the subject. As only one of several techniques, this method can be helpful. As a way of life, it is just as destructive as avoiding the issue. People soon learn that there is no sense in trying to resolve a conflict with this individual. He or she always manages to divert attention to some other issue or channel the energy in another direction. The ploy may work, but other staff members soon learn to bypass that person when dealing with problems.

Another technique is confrontation, either through power or negotiation. Let's look first at the former.

SCENE I

A secretary wants a clerk to do a job, but the clerk is reluctant to take on a new responsibility. The secretary not so gently reminds the clerk that an annual evaluation of work is due and that this refusal may result in a negative evaluation. Obviously, this is a power confrontation in which the clerk has limited options. Therefore, the clerk will bow to the secretary's power and do the job. However, since the reason for the refusal is never explored, the clerk will probably harbor ill feelings at being forced to do the work.

Let's take the same situation handled through a negotiating technique.

SCENE II

Another secretary approaches a clerk with the same job. When the clerk refuses to do the job, the secretary looks for the reason behind the refusal. She engages the clerk in conversation to try to determine why the clerk is reluctant to do the job.

The clerk has the chance to voice objections; the secretary has the opportunity to explain why it is necessary for her to assign this new duty. Through this communication process the conflict is brought out in the open in a productive problem-solving manner. This line of approach helps both participants to explore reasons, options, and alternatives. As a result, the secretary has an opportunity to reassess the action and the clerk has an opportunity to agree to the new responsibility. The issue becomes a problem to be solved by both. The conflict can be settled jointly, with both sides gaining insight to the other's point of view.

Both secretaries approached the conflict by confrontation, one through the use of power and one through the use of negotiation. It is not hard to see which technique will bring the greater rewards. Power brings agreement coupled with resentment. Negotiation brings communication and shared problem solving, giving both parties the chance to become involved in a mutually agreeable solution.

The diagram below illustrates the principle that conflict handled in a productive manner can be an asset to the office.

THE	handled	POWER		results	RELUCTANT
ISSUE	through	CONFRONTATION	in		AGREEMENT OR
					REFUSAL
THE	handled	NEGOTIATION		results	UNDERSTANDING,
ISSUE	through	CONFRONTATION	in		AGREEMENT,
					HARMONY

When a conflict is faced, the participants have an opportunity to negotiate a change leading to improved harmony. For example, consider the following scene.

SCENE

Mary has been the supervising secretary in her office for several years. When she started working, she had specific duties for her position. Over the years the range of responsibilities has increased; the number of clerical staff people reporting to her has not. Mary is faced with a heavier workload but the same amount of staff.

She has tried meeting with her administrator, but each time she feels that the timing is wrong and she has not received enough attention. She is at the boiling point, seriously considering quitting or asking for a transfer to another office.

The situation is undoubtedly leading to a conflict. The question is whether the technique will be avoidance (getting out) or negotiation confrontation. Mary is facing a crunch and has to make a choice.

If she decides not to do anything about it and weather the storm, Mary may believe that she has not made a decision, but putting off a decision is the same as deciding to do nothing.

Or, she may blow up on a day when everything goes wrong, demand extra help, most likely have her request denied, and then have the choice of either backing down and staying or leaving a job that she basically likes. With ultimatums the chances are always great that one will lose. And even if the administrator agrees to the demands, the administrator may look upon Mary in a negative light in the future.

Or, Mary could face the conflict with planned negotiations. She could ask to meet with her administrator, document the workload, point out the need for additional help, and present a plan to the administrator. In essence, Mary could seek productive solutions. Confrontation negotiation provides more opportunities for success. In addition, by facing the conflict, Mary gains greater respect for her own ability to confront conflict and resolve it in a productive manner.

OPTIONS IN DEALING WITH CONFLICT

Conflict in the office is sometimes viewed from a different perspective in which each party to the confrontation makes choices from several behavior styles. Thomas and Kilmann [1] view conflict situations in terms of five behaviors: avoiding, competing, sharing, accommodating, and collaborating. The application in the school office is incredibly on target.

SCENE I

Behavior style: competing. Results: someone wins, someone loses.

A newly assigned secretary is delighted about the assignment. He has recently taken classes on office management and supervision and has a strong desire to put the knowledge to work.

On the other hand, the principal has been at the school a long time. Although he acknowledges that the clerical staff could use some new techniques, and some discipline in terms of signing in and out and following rules, the principal is reluctant to rock the boat.

He tries to be open minded and listens to the secretary's ideas, but ends the conversation by telling him to leave things alone. The secretary persists, trying to point out logically what would be gained. The administrator listens again, but says no.

As the secretary tries one more time, the principal slams his fist on the desk and shouts, "You'll do it my way. I am not interested in your suggestions. I run this school and you'll do it my way. Do you understand?"

The secretary, taken aback, says, "Yes," and leaves.

Was there a conflict? Obviously there was. Was there a winner? Yes, the principal. Was there a loser? No doubt the secretary. Patently a win/lose situation.

What are the benefits? Discussion is ceased, the decision is made, and the subject is ended.

---

[1] *Thomas-Kilmann Conflict Mode Instrument* (Sterling Forest, Tuxedo, N.Y.: Xicom, Inc.).

What are the costs? The secretary will not suggest improvements again. He will probably be very leery of his new boss. And the clerical staff will continue with poor methods and bad habits.

Perhaps in this situation it is too kind to say that the principal won. In practice, probably both sides lost. But it is one way to approach conflict.

Here is another approach.

SCENE II

Behavior style: avoiding. Results: no one wins.

The secretary knows that one of the clerks, Mary, comes in ten minutes late every day. She knows she should speak to her, but keeps avoiding it.

The clerk also knows she is late. Further, she would like the opportunity to talk to the secretary. One of her children is having problems in school, and she would love the chance to share the problems, get some advice, and, more importantly, gain the support of the secretary. But the secretary is so hard to approach that she just keeps waiting.

Every day Mary comes in late. And every day the secretary looks the other way.

The secretary believes Mary is late intentionally. Since she does not face the issue, but avoids it, she is left with her imagination rather than the facts.

Mary, on the other hand, feels that perhaps if she does not broach the subject she will not get reprimanded. Although she feels she would be better off if she confided in the secretary, she is too insecure and feels that it is better to leave well enough alone.

Who wins? No one. The secretary assumes things about Mary and sets a bad example for the other clerks (who may begin to think coming in late is acceptable behavior), yet lacks the courage to approach her because she is afraid of a scene. Moreover, the secretary has always hated to supervise, and this is a supervision problem. Her perception of her own supervisory ability is diminished even further. Mary loses too, because although she avoids the confrontation, she is left worrying about what will happen if the secretary ever does confront her, and what will happen to her record as a clerk. She also feels inadequate because she does not face the issue.

Of course, avoiding the situation is costly. The secretary loses in terms of her leadership role as secretary, and Mary loses in terms of her future with the school.

Let's look at another way of approaching conflict.

SCENE III

Behavior style: accommodating. Results: one loses, one wins.

The teachers at the local junior high school drop off work in the main office each morning. One particular teacher does not organize the material, leaves hastily written instructions, and always needs the work at the last minute.

Jim has been getting annoyed at this teacher. He feels she is unfair in her attitude. He approaches her to talk. The teacher smiles, compliments Jim on the way he types the material, and proceeds to drop off another batch of hastily prepared, poorly organized material.

Jim is really furious, but is afraid to speak to the teacher about it. So, he smiles, jokes with the teacher, and tells her to stop by later that morning; the work will be done. The teacher, smiling, thanks Jim for being such a good sport, and leaves.

Who won? Well, Jim certainly did not. Not only is he left doing the work, but he also feels that he lacks backbone. He feels very unhappy about his responses to this teacher.

The teacher is really feeling great. Jim is saving her again and she is delighted.

Jim: 0; Teacher: 100. Surely an unfair resolution to a conflict.

So far we have explored three styles of dealing with conflict: competing, avoiding, and accommodating. Each is a recognized way of facing the issue, but each has a penalty.

There are two other methods that can be adopted, both giving participants a better chance at success.

SCENE IV

Behavior style: sharing. Results: half the time one person wins, half the time the other person wins.

John and Ann share a busy office. The five phones, which ring constantly, really drive them crazy.

Two students are assigned to help them. Since John and Ann each view training the students in a different way, they decide to share responsibility and training—each will train one. They assume that if each teaches one student his or her own method, peace will prevail.

On the surface, this may seem quite equitable—sharing 50/50.
But look at it in another light.

Ann will not like the way John's student is trained, nor will John appreciate the way Ann's student operates. Not only will both be frustrated when they must turn to the other student for help; they will also be more critical of the other's method because they did not subscribe to it.

Obviously 50/50 is fraught with problems. Another way of looking at it is that 50 percent of the time you win, and 50 percent of the time you lose.

Now let us look at another method of dealing with conflict using the same situation.

SCENE V

Behavior: collaborating. Results: both win.

John and Ann share an office and have the responsibility of training two students. Because each views the responsibilities in a different way, they sit down and separately draw up lists of what each feels the students should do.

After the lists are drafted, they work together to develop a composite list of responsibilities; further, they both work together in training the students. This way, they both win: 100/100. They work together to solve the conflict, the list reflects their needs, and both have a vested interest in its success.

Each of Thomas and Kilmann's five categories has some merit. Competing results in one person's getting his or her way; avoiding results in the problem's being totally avoided; accommodating creates one very happy person, although the other person comes out with nothing. Even sharing has its advantages and penalties, because the individual wins half the time and loses the other half.

It is only when we come to collaborating that both people come out winners. The solution is based on a consensus of what each can live with. In the process, each gets the opportunity to view the problem from the other's viewpoint, a very healthy step in the direction of solving all conflicts in a cooperative manner. However, keep in mind that different styles may be appropriate at different times. The point is that when facing conflicts people should consider a variety of behavior styles and use the one appropriate to the situation.

Is conflict inevitable in the school office? Obviously it is. The question is "Can productive methods be developed to deal with it?" As demonstrated, we believe the answer is a resounding, "Yes." With a little ingenuity and some patience, not only is conflict faced and the problem solved, but teamness is built. Each side shares and works together on the product, and each has a feeling of success.

ANGER AND THE OFFICE EMPLOYEE

In introducing the concept of conflict in school offices, we alluded to the myth that educational office employees face no conflicts in working with others. Closely aligned to the myth about conflict is one about anger—"Educational office employees are never angry." The latter myth is just as erroneous as the former. Ignoring anger can lead to similar consequences: poor morale, lack of communication, and diminished productivity.

Additionally, an interesting phenomenon occurs as a result of the way people handle anger. People are more responsive and sensitive to people who openly share anger than to those who pretend they are not angry. This occurs because the one who pretends he or she is not angry leaves no opportunity for others to help solve or alleviate the problem. By pretending no problem exists, the person closes the door to discussion. The person who is open about being angry is at least honest about the feeling, and people respond to that openness.

Let's first examine what occurs when an individual becomes angry. This will be followed by a discussion of methods of dealing with anger, whether you are the angry person or the person against whom the anger is directed. As a conclusion, typical situations that may create anger will be discussed and alternatives explored.

Just what causes an individual to feel angry?

Have you ever stood by in amazement as another office employee seethed at a comment? When you asked what happened, the response made reference to something that had not bothered you at all—in fact, if the person had not been so angry you might have been inclined to comment on how foolish it was to be angry over the incident.

Reflect on the last time you were angry. Chances are it was more a feeling of helplessness that triggered the anger, not the incident itself. Therein lies the beginning of the anger syndrome. According to Jones and Banet, when a situation engenders a feeling of powerlessness in the individual, it triggers anger. This powerlessness can be a common feeling in a school office where the support staff members are aware that their role is to serve, without question or challenge, even when they receive what is perceived as unfair treatment. Often the intensity of the anger is in direct relationship to the feeling of helplessness and vulnerability.

For example, the community member who presses too hard on the phone, the teacher who speaks in a condescending manner, the administrator who reprimands publicly—all may cause office staff members to feel they do not have the power to change the person or respond as they would like to the behavior.

If a staff member responds in a similarly aggressive manner, he or she will probably accelerate the abusive behavior, causing a lose/lose situation. But if nothing is said, the person who angers the office staff member may not even be aware of having done so.

Obviously anger is a state of mind, one which may not be shared by the initiator of the action provoking anger. Yet, if a feeling of powerlessness or vulnerability sparks the anger, the first step is to question what the angry individual can do to alleviate the strain and deal with the matter productively.

The second step is to analyze what triggered the cycle. Is the other person angry at you, or are you angry at the other person? This determination is critical if one is to develop an appropriate, productive means of dealing with the anger.

The third step is to determine where the anger comes from. Often when we feel angry because of the annoying actions of another we find that our own angry feelings were triggered by the belligerent behavior of the other person. Initially the other person is angry and owns the anger. However, in the process of sharing, it hit our "hot button" and we too become angry.

At first, one may want to retaliate, to get back at the culprit because he or she triggered anger in us. Here is where the treatment of anger must become sophisticated. We must look at the anger and determine alternatives to retaliation.

If the anger is initiated by another, we can take control of the situation and communicate in a positive manner. We can

> acknowledge that the other person appears angry
>
> share the perception that this must be a troublesome concern
>
> validate the person's feelings of anger
>
> suggest that we wish to discuss the issue in order to help solve the problem
>
> work with the individual to address concern and agree upon a solution
>
> check back to see if the concern is truly solved.

This technique may seem lengthy, but look at what happens. Obviously the anger of the other person was becoming contagious. You too were feeling angry, not because of something that initiated with you but because you were the recipient of the other's angry feeling.

By acknowledging the other person's anger, you are saying that you sense the anger and wish to do something about it. Contrast this to a confrontation, where each one ends up trying to top the other.

By validating the person's anger, you are also saying that he or she is important to you and you wish to help find a solution to something that is obviously troublesome.

Third, by taking the time to explore options, you are indicating that you much prefer solutions and closure to angry feelings.

And lastly, by checking back to see if the solution is indeed what was wanted, you can ensure that the person is still satisfied and that the situation will not escalate in the future.

It might sound like a lot of work, but consider the alternatives: either the other person is angry, you are angry, or both of you are angry. Solutions do not come easily in this milieu, especially when the office climate is one of tension, rather than tact and helping.

Now approach anger from the other side: you are angry. Something has happened that you perceive as a threat and you may not have the power to force the other person to do your bidding. This may trigger the "hot button" or the feeling of vulnerability. Your options seem to be fight or flight. Either option elicits negative results. Fight—you may lose, certainly your school comes out losing. Flight—you may never resolve the issue, it will only come back to haunt you at a later date. So look at some other options. How about affirming your anger?

The school secretary who believes one should never become angry may see this as a last alternative. But in fact it is often the best course to pursue.

One of the first steps in affirming is to acknowledge and own up to anger, but in a positive manner. When we discussed communication and assertiveness in the previous chapter, we mentioned "I" messages. Let's apply the same theory here.

If we say, "You made me angry," the other person would have to mount a defense by telling you what you did wrong. Or he or she could choose not to fight and suppress the feeling—only to take it out on the typewriter. We have all seen secretaries pounding on a typewriter to relieve tension and anger.

The "I" message solves the problem. When you affirm your anger using the "I" message, you share your perception of the problem. For example, suppose you feel another clerk in the office is not carrying her share of the workload. You speak to her about it, but she ignores you. Since you don't supervise her, you have no authority to delegate the work. Using an "I" message can open the door for discussion:

"I am upset and would like to speak to you about our workload. I can appreciate that you believe the work is equitably distributed, but I feel there is a difference. I'd like the opportunity to share my view with you and explore options."

The individual still can counteract your viewpoint by sharing his or her perception of the incident, but you have at least pointed out your concern and acknowledged your anger openly.

Just sharing anger is not enough. It is then critical to explore the reasons for your anger and what remedies you are seeking. To merely state that you are angry without offering some remedies leaves the other person in limbo: uncomfortable about knowing of the anger but with no options or alternatives for alleviating it. By sharing and seeking options, you are taking a positive approach to anger.

The third and final step is to agree on what will happen as a result of an understanding with the other person. So often we share our concern, decide what is needed to alleviate it, and then do not pursue the issue. Either party may then neglect to fulfill the agreement, leaving the other feeling unfulfilled and a little bitter. Therefore, closure must include an agreement to remedy the anger within a set time so both parties will know that the issue is closed. Of course, this method will not be necessary regarding some minor issue. But it is quite useful when the issue is one of enormous concern to you, one that has been bothering you for a long time. If the incident took a considerable amount of time to come to a head, it seems reasonable to expect that it may take a similar period of time to be fully rectified.

By checking back periodically both parties can ensure that when the issue is resolved, it will remain solved.

Working on anger in the school office takes patience and the skill of a negotiator. School secretaries are expected to have these talents, and working on anger will call upon every one of the skills the secretary possesses.

Yet this technique is not developed in isolation. Obviously any procedure like this requires the support and commitment of administration plus the people at work. Instituting a positive approach to anger in the office requires, perhaps even demands, that everyone agree with and support the system. Next time an incident arises, if you feel you wish to try out the system, you might preface your remarks by telling the staff that you feel angry and wish to share the anger with them in a new manner. Ask them to help you try this system. Involve them in adapting the system for themselves.

Once the system has been successful, it is not difficult to convert people to it. Everyone will enjoy being a part of the successful effort to deal with anger in the school office through the positive approach.

Figure 6–2

1. Conflict in the school office is_____

_____

2. When faced with a conflict in the school office, I_____

_____

3. If administrators challenge the procedures I use, I_____

_____

4. When I am angry, I_____

_____

5. People who are angry should_____

_____

6. When someone makes an unreasonable request, I_____

_____

Now that you have explored options for dealing with conflict and anger in the office, fill out Figure 6-2 and compare your responses to those for Figure 6-1, which you completed at the beginning of this chapter.

SUMMARY

Conflict and anger are two subjects that are generally viewed as inappropriate in school offices—the myth persists that they don't exist. Yet experience indicates that they are integral, if unwanted, behaviors that must be dealt with. The creative educational office employee can view each as providing opportunities for growth—to explore, expand, and enrich the communication process in the office.

In handling conflict, the aware office employee knows how to benefit from negotiation confrontation and avoid power confrontation. Moreover, he/she is knowledgeable about the various behavioral styles for dealing with conflict (compete, avoid, accommodate, share, and collaborate) and is able to select the technique that is most appropriate to the situation.

In handling anger, the educational office employee is aware that the myth that it doesn't exist is just that—and able to decide on a plan of action to make anger into a productive activity. This may involve either acknowledging the other person's anger and seeking the reason why or affirming his/her own anger and exploring the underlying causes. In either case, anger is channeled into activities to further communication and seek alternatives.

Anger and conflict, handled in a productive manner, can be catalysts that spur participants to embark on creative and innovative techniques, to explore new methods, and to discard stagnant and stultifying procedures. Creative anger and conflict can truly be a boon to the school secretary. They provide an opportunity for those involved to examine serious issues, analyze the problems, and apply the appropriate solution —all of which foster growth and change.

PROBLEMS

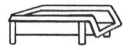

Problem 1

Grace is a new secretary. She is young and was recently graduated from secretarial school.

Barbara, the clerk, has been on the staff for five years and resents the new secretary. She feels Grace is too young and inexperienced and challenges her at every opportunity.

What advice would you give to Grace about handling this conflict?

Problem 2

According to Thomas and Kilmann, people approach differences in five ways:

    1 Avoiding
    2 Competing
    3 Sharing
    4 Accommodating
    5 Collaborating

Explore these styles and determine the benefits and detriments of each.

Problem 3

Sarah has been the office supervisor for five years. A new principal has been assigned, and she questions all of the procedures. Sarah feels threatened by the questions. She believes she is challenging her role as supervisor.

How should Sarah respond to her new administrator?

Bibliography

Dyer, Wayne. *Your Erroneous Zones*. New York: Funk & Wagnalls, 1976.

Jones, John E., and Banet, Anthony G., Jr. *Dealing with Anger: The 1976 Annual Handbook for Group Facilitators*. LaJolla, Calif.: University Associates, 1976.

Schmuck, Richard A., et al. *The Second Handbook of Organization Development in Schools*. Palo Alto, Calif.: Mayfield Publishing Co., 1977.

Stepsis, Joan A. "Conflict-Resolution Strategies," in *1974 Annual Handbook for Group Facilitators*. LaJolla, Calif.: University Associates, 1974.

Thomas-Kilmann Conflict Mode Instrument. Sterling Forest, Tuxedo, N.Y.: Xicom, Inc.

Chapter 7

A Positive Approach
to Public Relations

What one aspect of school management strikes terror in the heart of administration? Why, maintaining a positive public relations image, of course.

If the public relations posture is perceived in a positive manner, then a feeling of well-being toward the administration permeates the community. On the other hand, if this posture is viewed in a negative light, then very little that the administration does is viewed as constructive and a feeling of gloom may well hang over the school.

Although it is not absolute, the impact of a positive or negative public relations image cannot be taken lightly. With that emphasis in mind, we will focus on what is commonly known as the potent force in the public relations image of the local school: educational office staff.

The following list should help the reader focus on some common aspects of public relations. We suggest this be shared with other office staff members.

Has a procedure been developed for all office staff to follow when answering the telephone?

Are students who answer the phone trained in proper procedures?

Have you developed a procedure to follow when people are asked to wait on "hold"?

Does your administrator want you to screen calls? If so, do all staff members handle the process in a similar manner?

Have you determined a procedure for taking messages for teachers who receive phone calls?

Are emergency and commonly used numbers available immediately adjacent to each phone in the office?

Do you know what information (about students, events, etc.) may be given over the phone?

Is someone on staff available in the event a translator is needed (in a community that has multilingual needs)?

Have you set up a procedure to determine which office staff member has prime responsibility to take care of the office counter?

Is a bell available for visitors to use to gain the attention of the office staff in case they are busy with duties?

Are students trained to help people who enter the school office?

Are all written communications evaluated for their impact on public relations?

Is all material proofread in three ways in order to avoid communications with typographic errors?

Is the local newspaper kept informed about school activities and is publicity available to the community?

Since public relations is such a dynamic field, we feel certain that the reader can add additional items to the list.

In this chapter we will examine how the office staff demonstrates to the community and parents that the school cares about their concerns. The problems at the end of the chapter will pose a series of "what if's"— a compilation of the things that might possibly go wrong. We encourage the reader to brainstorm with members of the administrative and office staff for viable solutions.

Creativity and responsiveness to the needs of people are the by-words of public relations. If, when you must give parents an unfavorable answer, it is conveyed in a manner suggesting that their concerns are important and their needs are not being ignored, then a sound public relations program is in action.

TELEPHONE PROCEDURES

Telephone procedures cause one of the greatest problems in trying to maintain positive public relations. The reason is immediately apparent: the person at the other end of the line cannot see the educational office employee responding to the call and must imagine the facial expression, the gestures, and the feeling of the individual. Therefore, the caller uses the tone of voice and words of the staff member to judge how responsive the person is to the caller's concerns. This places a heavy burden on the educational office staff. Somehow they must convey in their tone and words that the callers are important and their concerns are of genuine interest to the school. No small task!

GREETING CALLERS

In order to provide this measure of warmth, educational office staffs have resorted to several techniques. They often open the conversation with "good morning" or "good afternoon." They identify themselves, and then, with a warm tone in their voice, seek to find out what the caller wants. However, with increasing numbers of calls into the office, this becomes time consuming. Often, too, "good morning" is still the greeting at three in the afternoon, causing the caller to wonder whether the employee is alert.

The telephone company has come up with an alternative which is being adapted throughout the country. They recommend that the salutation and greeting be eliminated. Instead, the office staff member should answer the phone in the following manner: "Jamestown School, Mary Jones."

The critical elements of a warm voice and helpful tone are supplied by the office employee. This is a sensible approach to conserving time, since a friendly voice can convey welcome and transmit the message of willingness to help. Although the elimination of the salutation streamlines the process and saves time, the warmth of the office employee continues to send out a positive image.

ACTIVITY

Discuss this concept with the school administrator and other members of the office staff. Since education is steeped in tradition, changing the method of answering the phone may well prompt feelings of concern. A call to your local phone company should validate that this technique is being recommended nationally. If your administrator decides to support the change, try to encourage all office employees to adopt the new method. By being consistent, the school presents an image of stability and continuity to the public.

SCREENING CALLERS

What's your policy on screening phone calls? No other issue raises as much controversy as this one. Feelings are generally polarized: for some, it is an effective time-saver; for others, it is a means of creating a barrier to the public. Let's look at both sides of the issue.

Screening calls can save time. Often, members of the public automatically ask for the principal or administrator. Since they are not familiar with the hierarchy in a school, they merely turn to the person at the top. By screening calls, office staff can ascertain what the needs of the caller are and transfer the call to the appropriate person. Calls that are meant for the principal are so routed.

Finding out who is calling can also save time in another way. While the call is being transferred to the administrator, the secretary can find any papers or documents needed to satisfactorily complete the call. Additionally, announcing the name of the caller to the principal gives him or her an opportunity to quickly prepare for the caller.

Screening calls also allows the secretary to hold calls or take messages until the administrator is available. To best manage time, busy administrators often curtail their outgoing and incoming calls to specific hours of the day so that they can reserve blocks of time when they can work undisturbed. They then return calls during specific periods of the day when the pace has lessened.

Yet despite the many timesaving reasons advanced in favor of screening calls, it is probably one of the greatest detractors to a sound public relations posture. Look at the negatives.

Often the parents and community perceive the school and its staff as distant, unfriendly, and elite. Approaching the school or calling the office is viewed by some as a necessary evil in order to get answers they need. When the administrator has a screening process, the caller's feelings of animosity to the school may increase. Therefore, any process that helps to keep that barrier intact works as a deterrent to good public relations.

When the caller is asked to state his or her name and reason for calling, he or she may feel that only important issues, as decreed by the administrator, will get through the screening. Even if the caller is transferred through, the feeling of having had to pass an examination remains. The caller is left with the thought: "I got through that time. Will I make it the next?"

In addition to the negative feelings it engenders in the caller about his or her worth, it creates an image that the administrator sits in judgment of or is better than the caller. The caller does not have the luxury of deciding whether or not he or she wishes to speak with the school. When someone from the school office or a teacher calls a parent, the parent is expected to respond. This lack of equality in expected responses intensifies the negative feelings of the caller.

Obviously, our position is that screening calls serves as a barrier between the caller and the administrative staff, a barrier that the people in education cannot afford to have.

Yet this discussion becomes academic if the administrator wants all phone calls screened.

ACTIVITY

Discuss the pros and cons of screening calls. Point out to the administrator that despite the timesaving quality of the approach, the public generally perceives it in a negative light, as one more barrier between the community and the administrator.

Keep a tally of the responses that are received when calls are screened. Be impartial. Describe how people respond to the screening process and share this information with the administrative staff.

Meet with the other members of the educational office staff to discuss the screening process. What has been their experience? How has it been received by the public? What negative responses have they received?

Suggest that the administrative staff forego screening calls for a period of time to determine if it really saves that much time when balanced against the positive feeling that the public experiences. After all, someone who feels that his or her concerns will be quickly addressed is apt to take less time over the phone than someone who has gone through the screening process, is angered by it, and is thus difficult to deal with.

If, despite your suggestions and your sharing of the comments, your administrator feels strongly that the screening process should continue, evaluate various techniques to reduce the resentment of people who find their calls being screened.

ACTIVITY

If, upon answering the phone, the secretary responds: "Yes, he is in. May I tell him who is calling?" the caller will not feel as if he or she is being screened, for it has been established that the person he or she is seeking is available. Finding out who is calling will then only serve to expedite the call. This procedure may help overcome the feeling that only the right people get through. By clarifying initially that the person is available, the secretary paves the way for the person to feel comfortable about the identification process.

ACTIVITY

Practice with other members of the team to perfect a tone to indicate to the caller that he or she is important. Often, the request for the caller's name may convey that the person is not important. While this may not be the intention of the office staff member, unfortunately it is the perception of many callers. By practicing with each other, the educational office staff members can develop a tone of warmth and support, reducing the potential negativism of screening calls.

If, despite all these efforts, some people refuse to give names, what are the options? This is an area to explore with the administrator. Although there are schools of thought recommending that callers must give names before being put through, this is inimical to developing good public relations. Therefore, we strongly recommend that even if the person refuses to give his or her name, the individual still be connected with the desired person. In situations like this, it is critical that annoyance not creep into the voice of the office staff member, even if the caller is rude. It is at times like these that the educational office employee may find it the most difficult to support the public relations image you are striving so hard to achieve. Sharing one's anger with other staff members may prove helpful. After all, it may be your turn today and theirs tomorrow. Supporting one another through the rough days will help everyone achieve sound public relations.

Another way of creating support is to be mindful of the screening problem faced by all office employees whenever calls are made to other offices. Each time you call another office, why not respond to the greeting by immediately identifying yourself and then requesting the name of the person with whom you wish to be connected? This way, screening is not needed. If this becomes a habit practiced by everyone, the problem of screening calls would soon be a thing of the past.

Additionally, don't overlook your assertive communication techniques. Whether you are dealing with someone who refuses to give his/her name or an individual who is rude and uses abusive language, assertiveness is a potent tool.

First, affirm the anger and frustration you hear in the caller's voice and message.

Second, validate that from his/her point of view, the issue is very troublesome.

Third, state what you would like to do to try to help alleviate the problem.

Fourth, ask for details and names so you can refer the person to the administrator who has responsibility in that area.

Communicating in an assertive manner conveys to the caller that you are competent, defuses the angry and frustrated feelings, and permits the caller to get attention without losing face.

ACTIVITY

Practice the assertive approach through role playing with office staff members. You play the role of the clerk, and have another staff member be the irate parent. Sit back to back during the scene so that you don't see the parent who is calling.

Then critique your performance. Were you assertive? Was the person satisfied with your response? Was the problem solved?

THE COUNTER—FRIEND OR FOE?

What does the counter in a school office mean to you? Does it convey an invitation, much like a Dutch door which is closed at the bottom but open halfway up in order to allow the person inside to greet visitors? Or does it look like an additional barrier? Is it a half wall that seems to say "Keep on the other side. You are not welcome beyond." In other words, is the school counter an invitation or a hurdle for the parents, community, students, and staff? The counter should bring welcome to those who approach it. They should always be greeted with a cheerful "May I help you?" and a positive posture and tone of voice.

Not everyone who enters the school office belongs on the school grounds, and not everyone is open and friendly. Therefore, we will be exploring ways of approaching distinctly different types of visitors without diminishing the public relations posture of the school. As every educational office staff member knows, this is not an easy task.

THE FRIENDLY VISITOR

The friendly visitor is the type of person who helps the office staff create a reputation for service and friendliness. She or he enters the office exuding self-confidence, approaches the counter in a friendly manner, is open to questions about identity, and makes requests clearly and concisely. Standard protocol does the job here; the individual usually leaves with the mission accomplished.

Even if the mission is to share a complaint, this individual does not interpret the problem as a putdown by the school administrators. By manner, he or she demonstrates an openness to suggestions and a reasonableness in requests.

THE TIMID VISITOR

The school staff can quickly read the timid visitor. He or she approaches the counter in a timid manner and may seem reluctant to disturb the staff. The person may search the eyes of the school secretary, seeking a look of welcome and approval. These individuals need to know, either by words or deed, that the office staff wants to help. This climate of approval is critical, because often the timid community members do not avail themselves of the services of the school. If past experiences were not pleasant, it may become their practice to avoid the school office.

Whatever the reason for the timidity, be it language barriers, cultural differences, or unfamiliarity with the system, the office staff must reduce the fears of these individuals and serve them in a supportive, nurturing manner. To accomplish this:

> Smile as you arise from your desk and walk to the counter.
>
> Speak in a reassuring way and provide a means to determine whether or not the person has understood your message.
>
> Convey a feeling of patience in order to allay the person's fears of bothering you.
>
> Explore beyond the initial request to determine exactly what the person wants. Often people who feel insecure are reluctant to state their needs outright. Patience and ingenuity are needed by the office staff to be certain that the timid visitor has really achieved the goal or request that brought him or her into the office.
>
> Close the conversation in a hospitable manner so that if the person has to call again, he or she will expect to be treated in a supportive, helpful manner.

THE AGGRESSIVE VISITOR

All the public relations skills of the educational office staff are needed in dealings with the aggressive visitor. Aggressive individuals may be impolite, rude, even abusive. They may or may not have legitimate concerns—it does not make any difference. They come in ready to challenge and fight. The school secretary's approach often influences the outcome of the encounter; therefore, it must be varied. It may move from being assertive to including sensing and counseling skills.

Although some people who enter the school office do not display good manners, this breach should never result in the office staff's acting in a similar vein. A technique for controling an aggressive person, without infringing on the individual's rights, is assertive communication and behavior. Consider the following scene.

SCENE

A parent enters the school office. She is shouting.

Parent: (Shouting) What's wrong with you people? Nobody seems to care about my child or me. I want to see the principal.

Secretary: I see you are upset. The principal is out of the office at a meeting. May I help you?

Parent: (Shouting even louder) Don't give me that. I don't care where she is. I want to see her now.

Secretary: I understand that you are upset. But the principal is not here now—and your shouting is upsetting the students. I would like to get you help. Please tell me the problem. Perhaps someone else can help you.

Parent: I will not be put off. I must see someone who has authority.

Secretary: I can see you are concerned. Please tell me the problem and I will get someone to help you. Perhaps if you come over to this table and sit down you can give me the information I need to get help for you.

Parent: Fine, but I need help now.

We can hear the reader now: "That sounds good on paper, but does it work in person?" The answer is a resounding "Yes." It works because it consistently acknowledges the need of the parent; it focuses on something both value—the well-being of the students; and it continues to echo the concerns of the parent.

First, the secretary acknowledged that the parent was upset. The worst thing to do with someone who is upset is to tell the person he or she has no reason to be upset. Whether the situation would be upsetting to anyone else is immaterial.

Secondly, the secretary kept reaffirming that the principal was not available. So, when the parent calmed down and was able to hear clearly (angry people often take longer to hear what is said to them), the message throughout the communication from the secretary was consistent. In essence, the secretary affirmed the person's anger, stated that the principal was not available, pointed out that the person's behavior was upsetting the children (something parents, office staff, and administrators alike will consider unfavorable), and continually offered to get help when the mother could share her concern.

Why does the system work? Because everything the secretary did was in support of the angry person. The secretary consistently acknowledged the other person's feelings. Additionally, after establishing that the parent had concerns, she drew attention to the well-being of the students and how shouting tended to upset them. The secretary forced the parent to view her behavior in terms of how it influenced the students. This change of focus helped place the control of the situation into the secretary's hands. This change of control is critical. As long as the parent is shouting, he or she controls the situation. When the secretary begins to control the situation, the parent can be moved away from the center of the office to a place where the concern can be explored. The process of moving also helps the parent focus on a new task, getting help, and leave behind the past task, shouting or yelling.

During the entire communication, the secretary maintained a moderate voice, a calm demeanor, strong eye contact, and erect posture; in other words, she was a picture of calm control.

If, in any way, the parent senses that the secretary is unsure of him or herself, it makes the secretary seem ineffective—not the person the parent wants to talk with. The demeanor of control emphasizes the message that sharing the problem is the first step toward solution. Assertive behavior conveys a message of calm, control, and efficiency. It is truly a school office member's greatest asset in time of emergency.

The unwelcome visitor

More and more, school personnel are realizing that not every person who enters the school grounds is a parent or community member. Occasionally the individual is someone who does not belong there, perhaps even someone who wishes to harm others—students or staff. The purpose of this section is not to suggest techniques to take the place of a sound safety and security program which should be instituted on the district and school level. What we hope to deliver are techniques that office staff may use to intercept a stranger on campus, convey to the person that he or she is being watched, and communicate the presence of an unwelcome visitor to other staff.

The standard opening of the office staff, "May I help you?" is a potent tool in approaching strangers on campus. Whether the interception takes place in the office, or on campus as you are walking to other locations, your tone must be strong, assertive, and controlling. These four words, properly stated, transmit many messages:

I am aware that you are there.

I have a responsibility to approach you.

I expect an answer to my question and am knowledgeable on how to proceed if I do not receive one.

Look at the approach. By walking up to a stranger and seeking to help him or her, you make eye contact. This means you can identify the stranger at a later time. In addition, you are awaiting a response, so the individual cannot proceed until a response is given. If the stranger does not respond, or mumbles, or says he or she just wants to walk across the campus, the office staff member can then state that strangers are not permitted on campus, and offer to escort the person to the office to speak to the administrator in charge. If the stranger refuses the request, the educational office employee should then proceed with an alternative means of apprehending the stranger. This alternative should be worked out with the administrative staff preceding the opening of school.

Unfortunately, strangers, especially those with ulterior or sinister motives, are being seen more and more on campuses. You may well wonder why this is part of public relations. Consider what happens when anything untoward happens on a school campus: the immediate response of the parents and community is that they have been let down by the school administrators.

A sensible security and safety program should be an integral part of the public relations of the school. Perhaps this awareness on the part of the educational office staff will help initiate the program. But whether or not the school has a general program, every educational office employee should have a plan in case he or she should meet an unwanted and unfriendly visitor on campus.

WRITTEN COMMUNICATIONS

Public relations wears many hats. Besides including telephone techniques and the welcoming of people in the schools and offices, public relations is a part of virtually all written communications emanating from the school office. Obviously this includes letters to parents and the community. However, have you considered that it also includes documents not usually viewed as typical public relations material?

Memos to other schools and offices give mute testimony to the value placed on the written word. Therefore, they should pass the same stringent tests that are used on communications to the home. Teachers constantly send home written material with the students. These, too, convey a message. Therefore, they should receive the same scrutiny received by other messages to the home.

Needless to say, press releases must also pass this review. The local school is dependent on the newspaper to publicize events. Poorly prepared copy may wind up in the wastebasket and not on the front page.

Evidently, written communications convey more than just the written message. It is of prime importance to develop guidelines for school office staff in order to maintain a superior school image.

GRAMMAR

Although no attempt will be made here to teach business English and grammar (see the annotated bibliography for reference books), we do wish to emphasize this crucial aspect in public relations. Any communication with grammatical errors raises concern in the reader: the writer seems careless or lacking in knowledge. Parents are faced with the dilemma of entrusting their children to a school in which the administrative and teaching staffs do not seem to be versed in proper grammar usage.

Educational office employees must view this as a segment of their responsibilities. Styles change, rules may vary, and often the certified staff has not kept abreast of the changes. Or, as may happen, grammar may not be a strength. Instead of belaboring whose responsibility it is, the educational office staff should provide the expertise needed.

Listed below are some areas in which grammatical errors commonly occur. This list does not pretend to be all inclusive, but it is offered as a beginning. What other common grammatical errors can you think of?

gerunds

parallel use of verbs

agreement of subject and verb as to number

when to use who and whom

the proper usage of lie and lay

Although technically not grammatical in nature, other areas that should be watched are the following:

Changes in spelling rules; e.g., canceled not cancelled.

Changes in punctuation; e.g., the elimination of the second comma in typing a series of three items.

Changes in letter forms; e.g., the move to the simplified block letter so that the typist does not have to worry about whether the person addressed is a Mrs., Miss, or Ms.

Possessives, prepositions, and pronouns, the three P's that indicate how well informed the office staff is.

The proper use of grammar in written communications contributes, however subtly, to the public relations image of the school. If it is without fault, no one notices; if it is with error, then each member of the school family is judged as being less than he or she should be. It is up to the educational office staff to safeguard this critical element in public relations.

TONE

Defining the tone in written communications can be elusive, if not downright impossible. In speaking, the tone of the speaker's words is easy to identify. Inflection, pauses, and intonation all contribute to the way the listener receives the message and interprets it.

In writing, tone is not so easy to identify. In essence, the text should suggest support, caring, and empathy to the reader. The writer should sound like someone who wishes to treat the recipient with respect, dignity, and equality. How do you determine if your written communications possess this quality?

ACTIVITY

Ask people from outside the office to read material sent home. These helpers can be PTA members, community members, teachers, and other support staff. Obviously this can be done only if the communication is not of a confidential nature. After the individuals have read the written communication, ask them to respond to the following questions: How does this writing make you feel? Did you feel good when you read it? Did you feel respected? What type of response would you want to give? Does it make you angry? Does it engender warm feelings in you?

If the reader responds that any part of the letter triggered negative feelings, go back and reread the communication silently. The parallel to speaking aloud is quite evident. Communications, even when read silently, cause the reader to mentally read with the same emphasis as if reading aloud.

If you feel this is farfetched, try a simple experiment. Pick up a communication conveying a negative message and read it silently to yourself. As you read the words, don't you find yourself providing tone in the way you mentally read? Without thinking, you add inflections, emphasis, and phrasing. People who receive your written communications provide this same emphasis. It will be up to the office staff to examine all written communications for tone. Many outstanding programs have gotten off to a poor start because the tone of the communication creates a barrier with the parents.

THE POSITIVE SANDWICH

Despite all the efforts of the educational staff to create a positive tone in the words used in their letters, sometimes bad news must be transmitted in written form. When a child has been suspended, summer school has been canceled, or a program is being eliminated, the office staff often must deliver the news. The challenge is to do so in a positive manner. The answer is the positive sandwich.

This technique involves nothing more than good old common sense. Approaching someone abruptly with negative news creates a negative feeling. Opening up a conversation with some positive aspect, following it with the bad news, and then closing with another positive aspect creates a sandwich around the bad news. It makes the bad news a little more palatable, but still gets the point across.

For instance, in a letter about canceling a program, if the opening paragraph highlights the gratitude for continued parent support, the second paragraph leads into the bad news about the cancellation, and the letter ends with the hope that future programs will receive the same support as the one canceled, parents get the bad news but also are recognized for the support they have provided the school.

Telling someone who applied for a job that it was given to someone else may be a difficult message to make positive. Yet praising the person for the skills demonstrated, explaining that someone else was selected because of experience more closely allied to the needs of the position, and closing with the acknowledgment that the individual's skills will certainly be appreciated in another position lets the person know that he or she was not selected, but leaves the individual with the feeling that he or she does, indeed, have worthwhile skills.

Obviously, the purpose of the positive sandwich is not to lie. Its purpose is to make bad news more palatable. In so doing, we recognize the feelings of others and treat them with dignity and care. Isn't that what good public relations is all about?

A final note on written communications: probably the most critical question to ask when preparing written material is "Is this letter or memo necessary?" Every written communication should be examined on the criterion of necessity. If it does not measure up, it should not be written.

SUMMARY

When we analyze the pros and cons of a positive public relations program, one critical element stands out. Good public relations helps the community, parents, and staff appreciate the contribution of office staff. Poor public relations clouds all these efforts and creates a barrier that hides this significant contribution from all those who benefit from it.

Developing effective public relations encompasses many factors.

The telephone is the number one image creator. Since the telephone is the means most commonly used by parents to reach the school, it is essential that all office staff members develop techniques to ensure that the phone constantly conveys a positive image.

The office itself is the next line of defense in safeguarding the school's image. The way visitors are greeted and the environment of the office both transmit a message. The knowledgeable office employee develops an office environment that sends out positive messages.

Visitors are a reality on any school campus. Most are welcome; some are not. The office staff must be sensitive to the needs of visitors who are seeking help, while being ever mindful of the safety of the students.

Finally, it is essential to realize that written communications may be a powerful tool in enforcing a good public relations image if they are handled well, and a potent detractor if they are handled incorrectly. Therefore, it is imperative that all written communications be analyzed and scrutinized to ensure that they convey the message that the school staff members are knowledgeable in English and writing skills.

Although effective public relations is often considered the province of the administrative staff, it is clear that a knowledgeable office staff can contribute significantly.

PROBLEMS

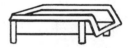

The positive public relations image we have been discussing is based on the ability to respond in a positive manner to the "what if's"— the potential problems in school offices. "What if's" are the fear of educational office staff. They are the unplanned for emergencies not listed in the book on emergencies, and the types of experiences that convince the staff they missed an opportunity by not staying home for the day.

We do not wish to take the "what if's" lightly. It was probably just these "what if" situations that caused the National Association of Educational Office Personnel to coin the phrase "Don't panic, adjust."

Therefore, we wish to look at some possible problems and encourage the reader to work with administrative and office staff to determine just what the approach should be.

Problem 1

It has been one of those days—students have been in and out of the office all day. It is now close to the end of the school day. Two children are ill and lying down. They begin to cry, claiming they are nauseous. At that point, an irate parent walks into the office with her crying daughter. The principal then appears at the office door with some unexpected statistical typing. Simultaneously the phone begins to ring and the fire bell goes off. What do you do first?

Problem 2

You are sitting at the switchboard. Most of the lines are in use. Another incoming call lights up. When you identify your school, the caller indicates there is a bomb on campus.

Enumerate the steps you take.

Problem 3

There have been a few problems with gangs. As the principal's secretary, you know something about many of the activities that have been causing concern.

The principal is out of the office and a call comes in from the local newspaper. They have heard about the rumors and wish to find out if a gang fight is expected that day. This particular writer has been giving your school bad writeups. You feel a need to respond. How do you? What do you say?

Problem 4

List some of the public relations problems that have occurred at your school. Working with other members of the office staff, enumerate the steps that were taken and then explore options to be used in the future.

Bibliography

Ferguson, Donald; Rowson, John; and Marx, Gary. *Making the Wheels Go Round in Public Relations.* Arlington, Va.: National Schools Public Relations Association, 1975.

Ferguson, Donald; Rowson, John; and Marx, Gary. *Your Office Staff: A Plus for School Public Relations.* Arlington, Va.: National Schools Public Relations Association, 1975.

Stewart, Marie M., et al. *Business English and Communication,* 4th ed. New York: McGraw-Hill, 1972.

Chapter 8

Student Workers

For the educational secretary, student workers can be either a gift or a headache. If the students contribute to the effectiveness of the office, the staff extols their virtues. But if the students create problems and take an undue amount of time, even the most patient office staff becomes disenchanted and resistant to student workers.

Student workers can be an enormous asset to the staff. In times of shrinking dollars and increased work load, they can provide free help. Additionally, the experience they gain in the office may open new career paths for them—they may be the paid school office staff of the future. Unfortunately, these assets go unseen by staff members who have taken precious time to train students who do not want to be there or have had students assigned to them as a form of punishment, not reward.

With this in mind, we choose to approach this chapter from the viewpoint of the optimist—the glass is half-full, not half-empty. Student workers can be assets, and we present practical techniques to help them become so.

Often a problem in utilizing student workers is lack of clarity in

Who does the selecting?
Who does the training?
Who does the supervising?
Who does the grading?

The supervision and training of students are fundamentally the province of the certified staff; teachers are ultimately responsible for instructing students. However, many of the particular responsibilities are often delegated to the office staff to be performed under the close supervision of a certified staff member.

Keeping legal responsibilities in mind, we will explore methods for working with students to make the experience meaningful, rewarding, and educational for everyone involved.

DEFINING THE JOB

Each position filled by student workers should have a job description defining the duties expected. This description serves several purposes:

1. It aids in the selection of the student.
2. It provides an outline of what is expected of the student.
3. It serves as one of the criteria for grading.
4. It gives guidance to the office staff on what skills the student should gain in the office.
5. It provides continuity from one semester to another. As new students move into the office, they have the same jobs to do as those leaving. In case of the departure of an office staff member, it orients the new office employees to what duties are expected of students.

The educational office employees must work with either the teaching or the administrative staff in compiling the descriptions. Make sure the ability and maturity level of the students are on a par with the duties to be learned. This is critical in working with elementary, junior, and even senior high school students. Admittedly, elementary students are seldom assigned regularly to school offices; if such were the case, the list of duties would need clearance from the teaching staff.

If the student is taking business courses, it may be wise for staff to share the job description with the business teachers involved to determine appropriateness. In addition, the office staff may be able to work cooperatively with the business education teachers in providing meaningful experiences building on the lessons currently being taught.

Obviously, the compiling of a job description for students creates an additional responsibility for what might be an overburdened office staff. Thus, the description may have to be only a guideline—or perhaps be compiled by the students. Despite limitations, we strongly recommend that some guidelines be developed and shared with the student.

The job description for student workers takes on the same significance as the one provided for the office staff. It serves as a guide to achievement. With it, goals are achievable; without it, progress is difficult to measure.

SELECTING THE STUDENTS

The selection of student workers is and should be the responsibility of the certified staff. Yet since the office employees are so closely involved with the student workers, it is not inappropriate for them to speak to the people who have this responsibility prior to the selection of students.

The office secretary can draw a profile of the type of student most likely to have a meaningful learning experience in the office. Areas to discuss include:

What skills will the student need to be successful?

Is a knowledge of the switchboard necessary, or will that training be provided?

Is clarity of speech and diction an important factor?

Will the student be expected to know the names of the teachers, administrators, and staff, or is there time to train the individual?

On the surface, these questions may appear to screen people out rather than approve their assignment. But assigning people who are prepared will improve their opportunities to learn and grow on the job.

Although being a student worker does not provide any pay, it is comparable to having a regular job. Even though office staff will train the student in specific duties, screening is crucial to determine if the students can perform the job satisfactorily. The screening process is no less important here than when office staff members are being hired.

Many problems arise in the area of selection. Because office needs are not always shared with the counseling or certified staff who do the assigning, students are placed who do not have the prerequisites necessary for work to be a worthwhile learning experience. By sharing this information, the educational office staff can contribute to the success of the experience for the student workers.

TRAINING THE STUDENTS

Teaching students is the province of the teaching and administrative staff. However, educational office staff members often perform these duties under the supervision of the certified staff. By creating a training program, in conjunction with the teaching staff, office staff could aid in developing students who truly help in the office and thus avoid just "baby-sitting" bored students.

On the other hand, nothing is more demoralizing to a student than to spend a semester running errands and never learning anything new. In addition, if many students have this experience, it will become increasingly difficult to recruit people, since word will go round that the job is boring. Making the students' jobs challenging not only gives the office staff additional help, but ensures a ready supply of competent students for subsequent semesters. A sound training program will serve both groups, the educational office staff and the students.

Training students is very similar to training new employees. The same atmosphere of support, patience, and understanding is needed, perhaps in even greater abundance.

The office staff must be ever mindful of the maturity level of the trainee. Often what may appear to be reluctance to do a task may be inability to do it. Since students mature at different levels, the office personnel must work carefully with the certified staff in the event there are difficulties in the training process.

Look at the week prior to the first day of the semester as the first step in the training process. Explore with administration whether it would be possible to have an orientation session with the students who are to be assigned to the office as student workers. At the orientation session, which will certainly be less hectic than the first week of school, the guidelines for office decorum, the list of job responsibilities, and the measurement of learning should be discussed with the students. This critical step serves as a baseline for the entire semester. Students should be given a folder with the following information:

Job responsibilities
Office protocol
Bell schedules
Lists of faculty, administrative, and support staff members
Pictures of the staff members (This can be developed if school pictures are taken yearly.)
Telephone procedures
Telephone numbers in case of emergency.

This folder serves several functions: it provides a framework for the job; it indicates to the students that their responsibilities are not viewed lightly by the staff; and it provides a security blanket during the first hectic weeks of school, when the office staff may be very busy and unable to provide answers to every question that arises.

Even if this orientation must be held the first week of the semester, be sure it takes place.

The training process for students is similar to the one described in Chapter 5.

Describe the task.
Demonstrate the task.

Have the person perform the task under supervision.

Give the individual the opportunity to perform it alone, but be available for questions.

Evaluate the performance, giving instructions if the task was not done properly and giving praise on the effort expended, whether successful or not.

Continue to monitor and be available to help, as needed.

Provide feedback on performance. Tell the person of areas for improvement and areas of success.

Whether the task is filing, stacking books on shelves, answering the switchboard, reproducing material, typing, serving at the counter, or any of the hundreds of other tasks that keep a school office running smoothly, a training process gives students the satisfaction of learning to perform the task in a successful manner.

The significance of the training program is demonstrated at grading time. If students are graded on performance in the office, in essence the trainer is also being evaluated. Therefore, office staff should make sure that the training program achieves its goals.

DEVELOPING A DESK MANUAL

Accepting the concept that each position in a school office should have a desk or job manual to provide continuity for the staff members who have the job, why not extend this to the student jobs? The job or desk manual is really the textbook for the class.

Using the job description or list of duties as a guideline, develop a desk manual in order to instruct the students on the "how to's" of doing the job. What they are to do and how they are expected to do it should be included, as well as a copy of the material found in the orientation folder.

Since the office staff is probably overburdened, how can one find time to develop the book? Here students who have already worked in the office can be a help. Ask them to gather the material that has been useful to them in performing the job. Working as a team, the office staff and the students can determine exactly what supportive material is needed for the student to perform in an exemplary manner. This experience can be meaningful for students. It will also give the office staff insight into how students perceive their duties.

OFFICE PROTOCOL AND MANNERS

Often working in the school office is the student's introduction to the world of work. Staff members serve as role models, demonstrating the right and wrong of office procedures. Thus, telephone techniques, counter service, communications to the home, and treatment of other students all have significant effects on the student. Your answering the telephone in anger or haste conveys to the student that this is acceptable behavior. Therefore, the office staff members must recognize that they are under scrutiny and demonstrate proper procedures at all times.

How does the office staff ensure that students provide courteous service? Try asking the students how they would like to be treated when they enter the school office. Draw up a list of their suggestions in order to encourage them to provide such service to others. Students are often critical of the way they are treated. By asking them to develop the norms of how to treat people in the school office, you give them the opportunity to provide service to others in the same measure they wish it for themselves. This allows students to own the manners they display and it has a built-in monitoring system: their own feelings.

TELEPHONE PROCEDURES

Telephone procedures must be clearly explained to student workers, since the phone is the lifeblood of the school. People calling in are dependent on the person who answers that phone. This dependency makes it critical for the school office staff to train student workers to provide service beyond reproach. Although this is obviously part of the training program, we feel it is worthy of special recognition.

The training for students who answer the phone must go beyond the technicalities of transferring calls and referring to the proper parties. The areas most often criticized are the initial contact and response to the person calling in. Therefore, let's look at the entire process.

The first step is for the student to learn how the system works. If the system consists of a switchboard, then the local telephone company may provide assistance in training student workers as well as office employees on the proper procedures for taking incoming calls, transferring calls, and returning to the line. If this instruction is not readily available, it is up to the office staff to provide training. Often the business education teacher can provide valuable assistance in this process.

Yet the mechanics of answering the phone is but the first step. How this is done is what the public criticizes most. The voice level of students is often low. This may be because they are new to the system and are unsure of themselves, or they may just speak in subdued tones. Whatever the reason, they need to be made aware of how soft their voice sounds over the phone. By recording the student's voice as he or she answers the phone and then playing it back, you can give the student instant feedback on how well the voice projects.

Additionally, new student workers should be provided with a list of common responses appropriate for answering the phone. Often, students do not know what to say—a list of responses to commonly asked questions will help them respond to the needs of the caller. No one likes to respond by saying that he or she does not know the answer. It is rewarding for the student to have the means of answering most questions.

One good approach is to have students practice with each other. When phones are not busy, student workers can take turns calling the switchboard from extensions in the office. In this way, they can help each other gain insight into how their voice is heard over the phone and how they can improve their technique. When the criticisms and suggestions come from their peers, it may be easier for the students to accept and implement them. Additionally, this builds teamness among the student workers.

Another method is to call into the office on occasion to hear first-hand how the students are responding to callers and whether additional training is needed. You can monitor for voice level, clarity of speech, and appropriateness of response.

This will also give the educational office staff an opportunity to praise students using especially effective techniques and give guidance to those who are not. Remember, reinforcement of well-performed tasks through praise ensures that students will continue the exemplary performance. Giving guidance has positive as well as negative connotations. It suggests that you believe the student is capable and with the right information could improve upon the performance.

GRADING OF STUDENTS

Again, grading is the province of the teaching and administrative staff. However, we firmly believe that the educational office staff should be part of this process.

The grading process is the culmination of many steps. The selection, the job description, the orientation, the training, and the office protocol all help to pave the way for the grading. How can the educational office staff be involved in a way supportive of the student worker's progress without infringing on the legal rights and responsibilities of the teachers? Preplanning and communication are the answer. If the office staff and the teaching staff have worked together to set the guidelines for the student's behavior and how to measure it, then grading is merely the culmination of this process.

During the semester the office staff should keep a work record of the tasks performed by the student. This provides the teaching staff with a tangible measure of performance. Office staff should also meet with the appropriate teacher to provide further observations on performance. If appropriate, this can be followed by a joint meeting of student, teacher, and office supervisor to share with the student how the grade was determined.

Why get involved in this area when it is the teacher's responsibility? Because this is how the credibility of the office staff is reinforced. If students know that their performance was monitored and shared with the teacher, and that doing a good job was rewarded, they will transmit this information to incoming students. If this does not happen, students will come to see the office staff as unimportant. Additionally, this sharing helps to bridge the gap often experienced between support personnel and teachers.

Grading student workers is not unlike conducting a performance evaluation for subordinates. The same recognition of abilities and performance provides the subordinate and student alike with a knowledge of what is being evaluated, what is needed to do a good job, and how he or she can improve. It should be nothing less.

Figure 8-1 provides a checklist of factors that should be considered when using student workers. Share the list with your administrator to decide which are appropriate for your office.

Figure 8–1   Student Worker Checklist

Is there a job description for each student worker?

Have you met with the counseling staff to discuss what abilities and qualities prospective student workers should possess?

Do you plan an orientation meeting prior to the beginning of the semester to give the students an overview of their responsibilities?

Have you checked with a counselor or administrator to determine if the tasks enumerated are commensurate with the maturity level of the students involved?

Is your training program geared for success? Have you developed an atmosphere in which students can ask for additional help without feeling uncomfortable?

Figure 8–1 (*continued*)

Have you provided the students with the criteria on which they will be graded?

Did you meet with the certified staff member who will be grading the students so that you and he/she both understand the grading criteria?

Are students encouraged to help each other learn the tasks?

Do you regularly evaluate how well students are learning to be workers?

Do you involve students in developing desk job manuals to improve continuity from semester to semester?

SUMMARY

Student workers can be an enormous aid to the educational office staff. In addition, students gain hands-on experience in the office which may help mold their future goals. The student worker of today may well be the educational office employee of tomorrow.

Obviously, having student workers places a measure of responsibility on the office staff. Yet with the responsibility comes the pleasure of helping students have a meaningful learning experience in an atmosphere supportive of education.

There are several steps one should take to ensure that the student's experience is meaningful.

First, the job must be well defined. There is a close parallel between student workers and office staff members. Each must know what is expected. If a job description is not available, one should be developed by the office employee who supervises the student.

In addition, the office staff should provide information on the type of student to be selected. This can be through involvement in the actual selection or through development of a profile of qualities a student worker would need to possess in order to have a meaningful learning experience.

The training experience should parallel the procedure used with office staff—with safeguards to make sure that the level of responsibility and learning is commensurate with the student's ability.

In order to ensure continuity in student worker responsibility, the office supervisor should work with student workers to develop a desk manual. Attention must be given to office protocol and manners so that the student workers become aware of the norms required in an office environment. Further, office staff members need to be cognizant that their daily behavior provides role models for students; therefore it is essential that they model the procedures they expect the students to use.

Finally, policies must be formulated on how and when student workers answer the telephone.

One of the prime motivators prompting educational employees to seek employment in a school environment is the desire to be part of the educational process. Working with and training student workers brings this desire closer to reality and can be truly a rewarding experience.

PROBLEMS

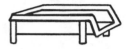

Problem 1

John Blake is a student in the junior high school. On occasion he has been sent to the office because of disciplinary problems. His teacher has suspended him from the class, and there is talk about assigning him to the school office as a student worker.

Discuss the ramifications of this transfer. How would you feel about it? How would you handle it?

Problem 2

Mary Brown is a young college student. She is working on a business degree and has asked to be assigned to the office as a student worker in order to learn office procedures.

Despite strong recommendations by the head of the business education department, Mary seems disinterested in working in the office and spends a great deal of time speaking with other students. She seldom completes her work.

What steps do you take to remedy the situation?

Problem 3

You have been the school secretary in a senior high school for several years. You have requested to have students assigned to the office, but the principal has been reluctant, especially when it comes to having students answer the phone. The principal seems to accept the concept but is worried about how students would affect the public relations image.

What steps can you take to convince the principal that the program is sound? Enumerate each step and develop an outline.

Chapter 9

Significant Legislation Affecting the Educational Office Employee

Perhaps one of the strongest examples of the expanding and changing role of the educational secretary is demonstrated by her or his involvement in the implementation of three significant pieces of federal legislation: Title VII (Affirmative Action), Title IX (Sex Equity), and the Family Educational Rights and Privacy Act.

Although the responsibility for the enforcement of these laws rests on the administrative staff, the enactment of district rules is often delegated to the educational office staff. Furthermore, the educational office staff members do influence—either positively or negatively—the enforcement of these laws. As they meet the public, the students, and the teachers, their behavior serves to uphold or deny these laws. Sometimes this influence is minimal; however, it can be significant and may limit an individual's rights. By being cognizant of the ramifications of these laws, the office staff will be better able to support the role and responsibilities of administration.

Since federal rules are often amended, we will not attempt to cite the latest language of the legislation. Instead our goal in this chapter is to heighten the awareness of school office employees of their responsibility to safeguard the rights of all who enter the school office.

As a first step in the awareness process, we ask you to respond to the questions in Figure 9-1 and cite the reasons for your choice.

Figure 9–1

1. When selecting a new clerk, do you ask the applicant about marital status?
   Answer and reason: _____

_____

Figure 9–1 (continued)

2. Do you inquire if there may be problems in securing baby-sitters?
   Answer and reason: _____

   _____

3. Are men eligible to be office employees?
   Answer and reason: _____

   _____

4. Have you examined the application forms to make sure that the questions are not biased or sexist?
   Answer and reason: _____

   _____

5. When giving assignments to student workers, do you differentiate responsibilities based solely on whether the person is male or female?
   Answer and reason: _____

   _____

6. Are you evaluating written communications to parents and staff to determine whether sexist language is being used?
   Answer and reason: _____

   _____

7. Are clerical members working in the counseling office aware of Title IX and Family Educational Rights and Privacy Act guidelines?
   Answer and reason: _____

   _____

8. Does the educational office employee who is responsible for distributing textbooks know which textbooks stereotype and offer suggestions on counteracting the stereotyping?
   Answer and reason: _____

   _____

9. Do you know how to evaluate textbooks and written communications to determine whether they contain descriptors that limit participation by virtue of sex?
   Answer and reason: _____

   _____

Figure 9–1 (continued)

10. Have you had meetings with members of the administrative staff to discuss how your district handles the release of information regarding students?
    Answer and reason: _____

    _____

11. Do you know what to do if a person comes into the office to request pupil records?
    Answer and reason: _____

    _____

12. Have you trained your office staff to be as knowledgeable as you about these significant pieces of legislation?
    Answer and reason: _____

    _____

13. Are student workers briefed on access to files, or, more important, files to which they should have no access?
    Answer and reason: _____

    _____

14. Does the system used to handle telephone inquiries regarding students both uphold the privacy act and keep public relations intact?
    Answer and reason: _____

    _____

Because two major concepts are being explored in this chapter— the first being sex equity and Affirmative Action, and the second being laws affecting release of information on pupils, we will address each subject separately.

SEX EQUITY AND AFFIRMATIVE ACTION

If, in the process of responding to the questionnaire, you found yourself wondering about the terminology or the meaning of sex stereo-typing, we encourage you to review the list of reference books at the end of the chapter or check with members of the counseling staff. In this chapter stereotyping refers to limiting of behavior and performance based on past practices, misperceptions, or labeling. In other words, stereotyping involves relying on expectations based on one person's belief about another without finding out if the expectations are true.

Perhaps examples of specific areas where stereotypes abound will help to clarify. Let's look at the issue of the selection of employees.

SELECTION OF EMPLOYEES

More and more, the educational office staff, and particularly the secretary, is becoming involved in the selection of the clerical staff. With this duty comes the responsibility to uphold the rights of potential employees. Specifically, interviews should be conducted in a manner supportive of affirmative action and Title IX—i.e., limits must not be placed on the individual just because of sex. Questions must be posed to both sexes and selection must not be based on whether the person is a man or woman.

In school offices, this question takes on a great deal of significance. Traditionally, the educational office staff has been female. If a man seeks a position in a school office, is he given the same opportunity to qualify as a woman or is his desire to work in a school office viewed as inappropriate, resulting in his not being seriously considered for the job? Conversely, are woman applicants asked questions about baby-sitting problems and children while male applicants are not? Treating men and women differently in the selection process is clearly a violation of equal opportunity rights.

Often people who discriminate argue that education is traditional and men in the office would be viewed as inappropriate. However, this argument does not work: first, because a majority of administrators are male, and second, because it is illegal to discriminate on the basis of sex. Additionally, schools should be in the forefront of modeling nondiscriminatory behavior. Sex stereotyping in a school office becomes a subtle yet pervasive influence on anyone who enters the school site.

Listed below are questions considered inappropriate in employee selection. Although some are not technically illegal, they do tend to limit the selection process and can be viewed as discriminatory.

1. How will you take care of your children? What will happen if they become ill?
2. Are you planning to get married soon?
3. What are your plans about having more children?
4. Will your husband mind if you work overtime?
5. There has never been a man in this job. Do you think you can handle it?

6. Our parents may object to a man. How will you handle that?
7. Our last clerk always came in early to make coffee. Would you mind doing that?

The list can go on and on.

What do all of these questions have in common? They tend to stereotype by virtue of sex, or they are posed to one sex and not another (questions 1, 3, 4, 5, 6).

We are sure you can add to the list. Sit down with members of the clerical staff and administrative staff and come up with lists of questions limiting selection. These should serve as guidelines of lines of questioning to avoid the next time an applicant is interviewed. In addition, check with your administrative offices. Generally someone can help you frame questions so they do not deny or abridge the applicants' rights.

There is another area where discrimination may exist: age discrimination. We are not talking about people over forty; we refer to the people under forty and more specifically to those in their early twenties and thirties.

Because of past practices and hiring traditions, many members of the office staff are women whose children are grown. As their mothering duties were reduced, they turned to the schools for employment. But changes in economics and lifestyles have changed the employment scene. As a result, younger men and women are seeking positions in school offices and are facing discrimination because of age: they are perceived as being too young.

For some reason, motherhood is viewed as a prerequisite for working with young people. "A sick child needs a woman in the office" is a view shared by many who do the selecting. Although this view is not applied to teachers, some justify it by saying that parents want their youngsters to be cared for by a "motherly" type of individual in the office.

To demonstrate how pervasive this view is, take a quick survey of your school and the neighboring schools. Do young adults work in the school offices? If not, is it because they do not apply or because they have been seen as inappropriate for the job? Perhaps selection at the district level has served as a barrier and these young people have been eliminated in the first wave of the process.

If young people are systematically eliminated from the selection process, either intentionally or unintentionally, the schools lose in many ways. The obvious loss is in the limitation on the number of people eligible for selection. Additionally, as we pointed out in Chapter 8, student workers are potential office employees for schools. But if the selection process eliminates the younger workers, the benefits of the training program will be reaped by another employer instead of the schools. In essence, equal opportunity legislation expands the pool of candidates, giving school administrators the opportunity to select from a more enriched and capable group.

As the reader can see, it is in the educational office employee's best interest to become informed and active in aiding the administrative staff in upholding equal opportunity legislation. The school secretary's knowledge in this area strengthens the administrative-office team. This can only result in enhanced service to the educational program.

NONTRADITIONAL CLASSES—
WHAT THE OFFICE STAFF SHOULD AND SHOULD NOT DO

Consider the counseling office in a secondary school or college. The student walks in, selects a class heretofore considered the province of the other sex, and turns to the office employee to say good-bye. The response, whether supportive or condemning, can greatly influence how the student performs in the class. Indeed, the response may even be responsible for the student's changing his or her mind about the selection.

Students should be treated nonjudgmentally by the office staff, whether they select traditional or nontraditional classes. While on the surface this may seem like common sense, in practice this is often difficult because nontraditional selections may challenge the office employee's own value system.

Boys who take homemaking may be viewed in a negative light. Girls who take shop classes may be considered to be lacking feminity. However, whatever the educational office staff member's value system, students have the right to make these selections and the office staff has the responsibility not to influence them negatively.

Students look to the office staff for an indication of approval. Therefore, it is vital for the educational office staff to work with counselors and administrative staff to learn about students' rights in class selection. Additionally, the two staffs should work as a team to develop office guidelines protecting these rights. Unfortunately, administrative staff, while aware of the law in terms of their own responsibilities, often does not see how the office staff must support these rules. Yet without sufficient knowledge, the office staff may undermine the counseling efforts without even being aware of doing so.

Therefore, the educational office staff members should take the initiative and request guidelines from the counseling staff so that they, too, are aware of Title IX regulations. This way, the bond between the administrative and office staffs is strengthened and the service to students is enhanced.

TEXTBOOKS THAT STEREOTYPE

Title IX does not mandate that textbooks in use be discarded, and due to budgetary restraints, most districts are not in a position to discard textbooks. However, printed materials do serve as subtle conveyors of stereotypical information. Therefore, it is up to the teacher to develop lesson plans around slanted material or use the material to highlight the way writing places restrictions on people based on their sex. It is here that the educational office employee who distributes the textbooks can be of help to the teaching staff.

Using reference material to determine which material is sexist, the textbook clerk can save teachers valuable time by sorting out which material is appropriate and which has to be used carefully. This service admittedly goes above and beyond the traditional role of storing textbooks and distributing them each semester. It involves the office staff in a supportive relationship with the teaching staff members without infringing on their domain of teaching students. Of course, teachers can choose whether or not to avail themselves of this service. But in any case it is important for the educational office employee to become aware of the nature of the textbooks being handled and be ready to be of service to the teachers, if requested. The elimination of sex stereotyping is a challenge for the entire educational community, including the office staff.

WRITTEN COMMUNICATIONS—DO THEY PASS THE TEST?

The written communications of a school or office are mute testimony to whether or not the concepts of affirmative action, Title IX, and equal opportunity are supported by the district. Letters, memos, and bulletins using words denoting sex roles diminish even the most forceful proclamation of the equal opportunity concept. This is particularly unfortunate since often the stereotypical message in no way reflects reality. Often the beliefs, attitudes, and behaviors demonstrated by staff are totally supportive. This dichotomy between what the communications convey and what policy really is creates a mixed message for the people who read the material. The educational office employee can contribute to a congruent message by monitoring written communications for sexism.

But just what is considered sexist language? What has been traditional and ongoing may now be illegal and improper. Listed below are

ways to avoid language that limits opportunities and perpetuates stereotypes.

> Avoid sexist salutations. Addressing letters to gentlemen runs the
> risk of offending women. Adopt the simplified letter style and the
> issue is avoided. In the simplified letter, the salutation is replaced
> by the subject line. Additionally, the closing is eliminated. This
> style is shown in Figure 9-2.

Figure 9–2   Simplified Letter Sample

Date

Jane Jones
17 Main Street
Anywhere, USA 00000

FORMAT FOR SIMPLIFIED LETTER

The format for the simplified letter is quite simple. All lines begin at
the left margin.

There are three spaces between the inside address and the subject line.
This is followed by three spaces to where the body of the letter begins.

This format, developed by the American Management Society, eliminates the need for salutations and complimentary closings. Additionally
the name of the writer is typed in solid capital letters five spaces below
the last sentence of the body of the letter.

This format helps to eliminate salutations limiting the gender of the
reader. Additionally, because of the solid block form, it eliminates the
need to set tabulations and thus speeds up the typing of the letter.

THE AUTHORS

Use appropriate and parallel titles. Women should not be referred to in terms of their marital relationships. Either eliminate the use of Mr. and Mrs. in written materials or substitute the term Ms. for Miss and Mrs. Women should be referred to the same way men are: both should be called by first or last name only, by their full name, or by title.

Reword sentences to eliminate masculine and feminine pronouns. An easy method is to use the plural form of pronouns and use plural verbs. If the plural use is inappropriate, the expression "he or she" will suffice.

Eliminate occupation terms denoting gender, such as foreman, salesman, mailman, and fireman. Substitute nonsexist titles such as supervisor, salesperson, mail carrier, and firefighter. These changes are especially significant in the counseling office or in any publication sent to parents and students.

Although, as before, the monitoring of these issues may technically be the province of the administrative and counseling staffs, the educational office employee is the one who types the communication. By being watchful and mindful of what constitutes sexist and biased writing, the school secretary can aid the certified staff in performing these duties. Laws change and so do mores and traditions. Thus we will not deal here with the specifics of Title IX and affirmative action. The purpose of this discussion is merely to raise your awareness of the concepts and suggest that many of the issues of sex equity and affirmative action affect the educational office staff members.

RELEASE OF INFORMATION ABOUT PUPILS

The Family Educational Rights and Privacy Act delineates the rights of students regarding privacy and confidentiality of educational records. Undoubtedly each school district has developed guidelines to aid site administrators in upholding this legislation. Our goal here is to develop specific techniques to aid the school office employees in performing their duties.

Step I: Review your district's written policy regarding the treatment of pupils' records and the release of information.

Step II: Read the forms and examine the record management steps and safeguards now in effect at your school.

Step III: Ask to meet with the administrator in charge of pupil records for a briefing on how the rules are enforced at your school. Note carefully the guidelines on student workers and their access to files.

Step IV: Meet with other members of the office staff to acquaint them with the rules affecting the privacy act and how it influences their responsibilities. Determine if their procedures are in line with district policies. Plan to meet again.

Step V: Explore areas in which procedures should be changed or strengthened at a subsequent meeting. Generate lists to share with administrators to determine how they want the changes handled.

Step VI: Meet with the office staff to finalize procedures for clerical involvement with the privacy act.

Step VII: Develop telephone techniques to enforce the privacy act without creating negative public relations for the school. When the administrative staff is not around, it often falls to the office staff to deny requests for information and indicate that an administrator will return the call. Unless treated considerately a demanding person may see this denial as an abridgment of his or her rights.

Step VIII: Check periodically to ensure that all members of the office staff are aware of the Family Educational Rights and Privacy Act and are correctly implementing district policies.

SUMMARY

Whether or not the issues of sex equity, affirmative action, and the Family Educational Rights and Privacy Act are legally the responsibility of the educational office staff is a mute point. By taking a position as a member of the administrative-office team, the school secretary accepts the responsibility to be knowledgeable in these areas.

Several steps should be taken to ensure that office procedures are in conformity with sex equity and affirmative action guidelines.

First, personnel selection procedures at the office or school site should be examined to ensure that they comply with guidelines. Additionally, office staff should be made aware that students have the right to select nontraditional classes and that they have a responsibility to be supportive when students make such selections. Although textbooks do not fall within the province of Title IX legislation, office employees with textbook responsibilities should know about which books support sex equity and which perpetuate stereotypical behavior. In that way they can keep teachers informed. Finally, written communications should be examined for sexist or stereotypical language. In addition, rules and procedures should be analyzed for language in order to eliminate the subtleties of biased language.

Insofar as the Family Educational Rights and Privacy Act is concerned, it is essential that the office staff members be aware of how district policies enforce the act. Each district develops rules to ensure legal compliance. Office staff should review these procedures to make sure the records management procedures comply with district rules. Even educational office employees whose responsibilities do not directly relate to the act should be made aware of the provisions of the act. Office employees who are affected should meet regularly to ensure that the guidelines are being enforced in areas for which they have responsibility.

By working with administration to develop methods and procedures to use their knowledge of the law, the educational office staff members have one more opportunity to demonstrate their abilities to be contributing members of the educational team.

PROBLEMS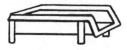

Problem 1

Mary Jones has just come for an interview. The position she is seeking is clerk typist in the main office of the high school.

The principal is impressed with Mary's qualifications but thinks she may be too old for the job. You are the school secretary and he has asked you to participate in the interview.

You are worried about whether Mary Jones will have her rights violated. How do you handle the situation?

Problem 2

You are the school secretary. As you walked by the counseling office, you overheard one of the clerks discouraging a young woman from entering an electric shop class. She said the class was "masculine."

Generally, you have left this clerk alone because her work performance is good. You are torn between interfering and upholding the rights of the student.

What steps can you take?

Problem 3

Develop guidelines for the office staff to help them become aware of the ramifications of Title IX and affirmative action legislation. Develop a checklist to aid the textbook clerk and teachers in determining if the textbooks tend to label and limit participation with sexist language.

Problem 4

As a new school secretary, you find that the handling of confidential information by the office staff is not consistent with your district's policy. However, there is resistance from the senior clerk when you try to raise the subject.

You know you need to reaffirm the rules, but are afraid to come on too strong.

What do you do?

Problem 5

You have approached the administrator in charge of pupil records to learn about how the Family Educational Rights and Privacy Act is implemented in your district. She seems reluctant to give you information and implies that it is not necessary for the office staff to know.

What steps do you take?

Problem 6

You have just been appointed school secretary in a school that is scheduled to open in three months.

Enumerate the steps you would take to set up and implement a records management system ensuring the enforcement of the district policy regarding the Family Educational Rights and Privacy Act.

Bibliography

Guidelines for Creating Positive Sexual and Racial Images in Educational Materials. New York: Macmillan Publishing Company, 1975.

Guidelines for Equal Treatment of the Sexes in McGraw-Hill Book Company Publications. New York: McGraw-Hill, no date.

Russell, Philip C. *Dynamic Job Interviewing for Women.* Port Hueneme, Calif.: Federally Employed Women, Inc., 1976.

Sabin, William A. *The Gregg Reference Manual,* 5th ed. New York: McGraw-Hill, 1977.

Sex Equality in Educational Administration, Vol. VII. Arlington, Va.: American Association of School Administrators, 1975.

Sex Equality in Educational Materials, Vol. IV. Arlington, Va.: American Association of School Administrators, 1975.

Sex Equality in School, Vol. V. Arlington, Va.: American Association of School Administrators, 1975.

Chapter 10

Time Management

> "If only I had more time, I could get organized. These interruptions just drive me crazy–"

Does this sound familiar? These words are echoed daily by countless educational office employees. Interruptions seem to come with the job.

There are 86,400 seconds in a day—no more, no less. Therefore, the request for additional time is one destined to go unfulfilled. Since the daily allotment of time is not negotiable just how does one get the most out of the 86,400 seconds available?

If you are typical, you have read information on time management for secretaries, applied it to your job, and found that many of the techniques do not work for you. It's not that the concepts are unsound, but that your responsibilities as an educational office employee are not typical. The problems are not the same, the pressures are not the same, and the clients are not the same.

Unfortunately, there has been a lack of appropriate time management techniques for the educational office. It is our hope to fill this void by presenting concepts and techniques developed with this staff in mind.

Time management is not a one-dimensional subject. In order to best use time, it is necessary to:

1. Determine whether you are a day person or a night person
2. Negotiate for time sharing
3. Determine whether you are oriented to people or to tasks
4. Determine control and no-control areas
5. Delegate and train subordinates
6. Develop daily, weekly, and monthly lists
7. Develop long-range work schedules
8. Organize desks and offices for maximum efficiency
9. Analyze reasons filing is neglected and develop timesaving techniques to solve the problem.

However, before exploring the effective use of time for the educational office staff, the reader is encouraged to complete a self-analysis of how time is currently being perceived and used (Figure 10-1).

Figure 10–1   Personal Analysis on the Use of Time

	YES	NO
1. At the end of the day, do you prepare a "to do" list for the next day?	___	___
2. Have you explored timesharing with other members of the office staff?	___	___
3. Do you know whether you are a morning or an afternoon person?	___	___
4. Do you develop time task calendars for major jobs and regularly occurring reports?	___	___
5. Have you worked out a schedule with your administrator to meet with him/her regularly?	___	___
6. Are you carrying too heavy a responsibility load while others on the staff are carrying too little?		
7. Have you met with your administrator to discuss your responsibilities and how you use time?	___	___
8. Are you doing any tasks that can be eliminated?	___	___
9. Have you delegated meaningful tasks to student workers?	___	___
10. Do you evaluate your time problems in terms of what you can control and what you cannot control?	___	___
11. Have you learned to laugh at the end of the day when, despite all your good planning and intentions, you could do nothing to maintain control over the use of your time?	___	___

ARE YOU AN A.M. OR P.M. PERSON?

Are you a morning or an afternoon person? Have you ever thought about it? The answer can be of enormous help in applying time management concepts.

Basically the morning person wakes up with enthusiasm, greets the day with a vigorous welcome, and works with energy early in the day. As the day proceeds, the energy level may waver. Generally, these people go to sleep early and awaken early the next day. Ask them about television shows that go on after 10 P.M. and they usually look at you blankly.

Conversely, the afternoon person is sluggish upon awakening and tends to take it easy early in the day. He or she picks up momentum as the day progresses and tends to be more productive later in the afternoon. Such individuals are usually well acquainted with television shows on after 10 P.M. and often bemoan how early schools open.

The significance in knowing your style lies in planning the workload. Morning people should plan on tending to complex responsibilities in the early part of the day, while afternoon people should look to the afternoon for greater productivity.

Unfortunately, school offices tend to be morning oriented. In the morning, teachers arrive needing supplies and services, students come to be readmitted, and parents stop in or call. Therefore, the individual who is more productive in the afternoon must be aware of this factor in order to compensate for the low energy level in the morning. However, when the morning people begin to slow down in the afternoon, and the afternoon rush comes on, the afternoon person will be able to pick up the slack.

Morning people face problems too. When the office quiets down in the afternoon and they have an opportunity to catch up on reports and paperwork, their energy level has dropped, along with accuracy; simple tasks become major hurdles as the day progresses.

Effective time managers are aware of whether they are morning or afternoon people. People who seem to have more time than others—and we know it is impossible—may simply have learned to tune in to when they are most effective and plan their more strenuous or mental activities accordingly. Additionally, they have discussed their morning or afternoon style with the people with whom they work, so they too can plan accordingly.

This cooperative approach to managing time leads to another concept: time sharing.

NEGOTIATING FOR TIME SHARING

Constant interruptions is one of the major time management problems cited by the educational office staff. Because of interruptions, office members have a difficult time blocking out periods of time to accomplish major tasks. They waste time taking out a project, trying to remember where they were when they put it away, restarting the task, and then having to stop because of yet another interruption. If this describes you, time sharing may be just what you need.

When blocks of time are needed to work on a time-consuming task, and there are two or more members of the office staff, work together to set up a schedule to take turns on the phone and at the counter. For example, consider the following scene.

SCENE

Jane and Mark both agree that one hour apiece of uninterrupted time would help them to work on major tasks and to make the most effective use of their time. Jane is a morning person and Mark is an afternoon person.

The Solution   Mark covers the phone and counter for Jane for an hour in the morning. Jane has a higher energy level then and can put the hour of uninterrupted time to use on major projects. At this time of the day she is most productive and accurate. Then in the afternoon, when Jane's energy level is reduced, she covers the phone and counter for Mark, who uses time more effectively in the afternoon. Since the administrative staff members are aware of their time management style, they lend support to the arrangement. Additionally, they try to plan their work loads to coincide with the higher energy level of Mark or Jane, as appropriate. This results in more accurate work and more satisfaction on the part of staff members who take pride in knowing their personal time needs are met.

The Dilemma   What if Jane and Mark are both morning or afternoon people? Then the productive time is shared on alternate days. By knowing when people are more productive, in the morning or afternoon, and developing time sharing methods to make use of this knowledge, the office staff makes better use of time.

PEOPLE ORIENTATION VERSUS TASK ORIENTATION

When an educational office employee is asked why she or he works in a school or administrative office, the response typically is "I like to be with people. I am people-oriented." Yet this very attribute often causes poor time utilization. For coupled with this desire to be of help to people is gratification at the positive feelings received from those who are the target of this people-oriented behavior. Simply put, educational secretaries receive positive reinforcement or "strokes" for being people-oriented and get little positive feedback for doing desk-oriented tasks well. They hear soon enough when the typing or reports are not correct, but seldom get positive reinforcement when the work is done flawlessly.

Interestingly, most job descriptions for educational office staff list the desk-oriented tasks, with only one or two lines mentioning the ability to get along with people. However, school administrators consistently state that one of the primary attributes they want in their office staff is proficiency in interpersonal skills—in other words, the ability to get along with others.

When it comes to the effective use of time, the educational office employee is caught in the middle between what she or he likes to do and is encouraged to do versus what the job description states must be done to perform adequately.

This dilemma has a profound effect on time management. When given a choice between people- or task-oriented work, staff members choose people-oriented responsibilities first. Yet time is typically allocated based on the job description focusing on the desk-oriented tasks.

A first step in dealing with this dilemma is to come to terms with whether you are people-oriented or task-oriented. A simple exercise will help.

Use Figure 10-2 to determine where you get the greatest job satisfaction.

Quickly jot down what satisfies and dissatisfies you at your job. Then go back and determine percentages of time allocated to each of these tasks.

Figure 10–2

Name of position			
Things I Do on My Job That Are Satisfying to Me	Percent of Time	Things I Do on My Job That Are Not Satisfying to Me	Percent of Time

Often the major time management problems emerge during this process. It becomes apparent that so much time is being allocated to people-oriented tasks that the desk-oriented tasks crucial to the running of the school are being neglected or relegated to secondary status.

To fully ascertain whether your initial evaluation is correct, keep a daily calendar of the way you are using time. Figure 10-3 may be adapted to your daily calendar. The purpose is to fully explore just how every

Figure 10–3   How I Use My Time

Name _____ Day _____ Date _____

What I Do (Be specific)   Administrator's Comment

8:00	
8:30	
9:00	
9:30	
10:00	
10:30	
11:00	
11:30	
12:00	
12:30	
1:00	
1:30	
2:00	
2:30	
3:00	
3:30	
4:00	
4:30	

day is being used. In order to make this meaningful, keep track of the use of time for one month. This way you will take into consideration the various monthly and weekly reports.

When this information has been gathered, ask to meet with your administrators and share the findings with them. It is now time for them to decide if they approve of how your time is being used.

If your time is being used primarily on people-oriented tasks and this use is acceptable to the administrative staff, then your road is clear. However, the administrative staff may feel a change in your use of time is in order. If the priority is changed you may have no control over the situation.

This leads to another aspect of time management—differing between control and no-control items.

CONTROL AND NO-CONTROL ITEMS

In time management seminars for educational office staff, a list of time wasters is generally developed. Before embarking on time effective techniques, it is necessary to determine if, in reality, the school secretary has any control over these time wasters. Quickly list what you perceive as time wasters on Figure 10-4. Then go back and check in the appro-

Figure 10–4

Time Wasters	Control	No Control

priate column whether you have any control over whether or not the time wasters occur.

Now go back and eliminate the no-control items from your list. There is no point in using energy and becoming aggravated over the no-control items. Of course, it is necessary to determine if they are really no-control items. For instance, being interrupted while doing a report is not really a no-control item if you have not made an effort to develop a time sharing procedure in your office.

Many people become so aggravated about the no-control items that they fail to plan wisely for the items they do control. You can gain control over the use of your time by focusing on the control items. One area in which to gain control is the use of the office staff.

DELEGATING RESPONSIBILITIES

If you have office staff or student workers, you are in a position to make effective use of your time. Go back and look at the time logs (Figure 10–3). Can you delegate anything on the list to other members of the office staff or student workers?

Often people do not delegate because they think either there is no time or the staff cannot do the job as well as they can. If you think the latter is the case, then serious analysis must be made of why the staff is not efficient. If lack of time is the only reason, then answer this: "How much time is it taking you to do the tasks?" Training would ensure that two people were available to do them in the future.

The time put into training subordinates and student workers is one of the best time investments an individual can make.

If you are reluctant to train subordinates you may be afraid of giving up control or of being dispensable. Only introspection can answer this. However, if subordinates and student workers have not been trained to take over some duties, it is time to face the issue.

There are many benefits to be derived from delegating responsibilities:

It relieves the school secretary of responsibilities so that she/he may use time in different ways

It keeps subordinates interested in the work, resulting in lower turnover rates

It provides a measure of stability to the office—if the secretary is out, others are able to fill in

It helps train subordinates to take on more responsible positions

It gives the school secretary the opportunity to learn newer and more responsible tasks—an area addressed in the next chapter.

The question still remains: "Where will you get the time to train staff and/or students?" Some ways of solving the problem:

time sharing with other offices

involving administrators and asking them to cover phones while you train personnel. It is in their interest also.

coming in early and staying late

using break time and lunch hours.

While we do not advocate the latter as a first choice, it may be the only way to get the job done. Be sure and check with your personnel office on prevailing laws.

So far we have focused on morning and afternoon people, the time sharing concept, people- versus task-orientation, differing control and no-control items, and delegation and training.

We are now ready to shift our emphasis to organizing time to achieve results.

DAILY, WEEKLY, AND MONTHLY LISTS

Supposedly, the concept of time management was developed around the turn of the century when an executive asked a consultant to help him better use his time. The consultant left and returned a short time later to make the following suggestions:

Make a list of all the things you want to accomplish in a given day. Determine which duties have greatest priority and work on them first. Each day redo the list and follow the procedure.

It is said the executive was so pleased that he gave the consultant $25,000, an enormous sum at that time.

The advice is still sound today. Making a plan for the use of time, determining priorities, and then sticking with them are still the most useful techniques there are. However, the use of lists can be applied not only to daily tasks, but to weekly, monthly, and yearly tasks.

DAILY LISTS

Figure 10-5 combines the daily task list with the administrator's calendar as well as with names of certified and classified substitutes. Obviously it can be amended for personal use.

We suggest adding yet another dimension to the list through use of colored pens or markers. For example, three things may have high priority, but one may be most critical. The use of colored ink can help the secretary to see it at a glance. The color key is

red: immediate attention
green: important—do today
blue: delegate to others
no color: do if time permits

Keep in mind that green can become a red because of change in priorities. And an area where no color is designated (do if time permits) can become a red item if neglected too long. For example, ordering supplies may be considered as having no priority. Then due to a sudden rush on a particular paper, it may become a priority item.

At the end of each day, the list is analyzed, incomplete tasks are written on the list for the next day, completed ones are checked off, and the next day's list is compiled.

The school secretary who develops this calendar for the school year can place payroll dates, report dates, and other items in appropriate places. Additionally, when the school secretary is out, the administrator can place notes on appropriate pages to keep the secretary informed.

Figure 10–5 Daily Schedule

		Day and Date
Appointments		
Time	Person	Materials Needed
———	———————	———————————
———	———————	———————————
———	———————	———————————
———	———————	———————————
———	———————	———————————
———	———————	———————————
———	———————	———————————

Figure 10–5 (*continued*)

Priority	Completed	Moved Forward to Next Day	Things to Do Today
_____	_____	_____	_____
_____	_____	_____	_____
_____	_____	_____	_____
_____	_____	_____	_____
_____	_____	_____	_____
_____	_____	_____	_____
_____	_____	_____	_____

Certified Substitutes	Employee No.	No. Hrs.	In Place of
_____	_____	_____	_____
_____	_____	_____	_____
_____	_____	_____	_____
_____	_____	_____	_____
_____	_____	_____	_____

Classified Substitutes	Employee No.	No. Hrs.	In Place of
_____	_____	_____	_____
_____	_____	_____	_____
_____	_____	_____	_____
_____	_____	_____	_____

WEEKLY LISTS

The items placed on the weekly lists usually consist of the tasks the school secretary wishes to accomplish during the week, but finds inappropriate to list under daily tasks. These are usually time-consuming activities which may take several days to complete:

cleaning the stock room

ordering supplies

conducting evaluations

cleaning files

Weekly lists serve as a master plan for accomplishing monthly duties that need to be planned and spaced throughout the month. Weekly tasks can be added to the bottom of the daily list calendar or on an additional page. By preparing weekly lists, the school secretary ensures that these tasks will be performed throughout the week and month and not left to pile up at the end of the month.

For example, attendance registers are generally prepared every four weeks. Waiting to order supplies until the same week registers are due is bound to put pressure on the office staff. Developing weekly lists prevents the backlog from occurring.

MONTHLY LISTS

The monthly lists, which may be part of the job procedure manual, are a compilation of major jobs and reports due. They guide the educational office secretary on how to manage time in the succeeding month. In essence, they serve as a tickler file (a file organized chronologically with lists of things to do) but with a major plus—samples of the reports are filed with the monthly calendar. Therefore, if a report on statistics is due, not only is this noted on the monthly report, but a sample of last year's report and instructions on how to compile it are filed with it.

Figure 10-6 may be of help in setting up the system.

Figure 10–6   Monthly List

_____

Month   Year

		Blank forms
Reports due	Date due	available in
1. _____	_____	_____
_____	_____	_____

Figure 10–6 *(continued)*

2. _____ _____ _____

   _____ _____ _____

3. _____ _____ _____

   _____ _____ _____

4. _____ _____ _____

   _____ _____ _____

5. _____ _____ _____

   _____ _____ _____

6. _____ _____ _____

   _____ _____ _____

7. _____ _____ _____

   _____ _____ _____

8. _____ _____ _____

   _____ _____ _____

School secretaries who are new to the educational environment often complain about the fact that it takes a full year to see a work cycle. This makes it difficult for new secretaries to project the use of their time. Using the monthly planning list to note reports will help the secretary plan for the future. In addition, if this system is in use at a school, new secretaries are able to review the lists of reports, study samples of previously submitted reports, and thus more easily meet deadlines.

DEVELOPING LONG-RANGE WORK SCHEDULES

Administrative staffs, because of the volume of responsibilities, are more and more often delegating the preparation of reports to the office secretary. The compilation of major complex reports is being added to the list of secretarial responsibilities. Because of the nature of the secretary's job, with its constant interruptions, it is necessary for the secretary to develop long-range plans and timelines in order to meet deadlines. Since deadlines are usually known, it is easiest to start with the final date and move backwards from there. In the process, interim deadlines are developed.

Let us use as an example a report due November 15, providing information on class size, teachers' schedules, and number of classes in each department of a secondary school.

The process: develop lists of the information needed and the people who must provide it. Determine how long each segment will take to be typed. Then fill in the Time Task Calendar (Figure 10-7).

Although the time task calendar may be used only sporadically throughout the year, it will help the educational secretary to better plan for major tasks. An added dividend occurs when the calendar is shared with all other members of the school team—teachers, administrators, and clerical staff. When deadlines approach, they can then understand the reason for adhering to them. In addition, clerical staff members, who may be called on to help when deadline time approaches, are able to plan their own time.

Daily, weekly, monthly, and time task calendars all contribute to the effective use of time. Yet this is still not enough. We must next look to the office environment to explore the way it influences the use of time.

ORGANIZING OFFICES FOR MAXIMUM EFFICIENCY

Often effective time management is seen strictly as a personal skill which people either have or strive for. We believe the efficient use of time is also dependent on the environment of the school—specifically the office. The best time management skills may be diminished if the office surroundings create barriers to full efficiency. Therefore, we must extend the time management concept to the office—in other words, what can you do to organize your office space for optimum use of time?

Efficient office management leads to effective time management in several ways:

Reduction in fatigue
Speed in movement
Improvement in morale

Figure 10-7 Time/Task Calendar

Classroom Report
Name of Report

Principal

Department Making Request

Inform Department
Chair at Faculty
Meeting Date
September 25

Distribute Form
Department Chair
Date
October 1

Analysis Time
Date Due
October 15

Typing Time
Date Due
November 1

Completion Date
November 15

November 15
Date Due

What elements are involved in effective office management?

Placement of office furniture
Type and arrangement of desks
Lighting and color of wall paint

PLACEMENT OF OFFICE FURNITURE

The placement of office furniture plays a particularly important role in the use of time. An analysis of work flow and communication patterns should be made to determine where desks should be placed. Although many school offices are limited in space and restricted by the counter, a work flow analysis will reveal if unnecessary steps are being taken or if too much time is being used in unnecessary tasks.

The process need not be complicated. Sketch a plan of the office as it currently stands and place it on a centrally located table. Each time someone moves to a different location, he or she marks the movement on the plan. Keep daily work flow charts for a week and then analyze for patterns. Two weeks later conduct a similar analysis. Repeating the process gives a long-range view of the work patterns.

Set aside a time to analyze the patterns in order to determine if the work flow is continuous and efficient. A poor work flow drains energy and time. The energy loss comes from unnecessary steps, and the time loss comes from slowing down the job. Unnecessary activity also creates more noise. This often results in further inefficiency and fatigue.

Also, check to see if desks are facing the wrong way. When two desks are facing, it is easier for people to chat. While this may improve morale, it may have a severe effect on productivity and use of time. Doing a work flow analysis helps bring these issues to the surface.

Several reference books cited in the Bibliography provide detailed information on analyzing work flow. Or, the reader may wish to develop a simplified form indicating each individual's activities and communication flow for several days. The time invested will be minimal when compared with the improved efficiency achieved.

One final word: it may seem sensible at first to discourage all unnecessary movement or noise in the office. Actually this is not wise. In the book *Maximum Performance,* Laurence Morehouse discusses fatigue in the office. He points out that total lack of movement reduces the energy level and results in less productivity. Additionally, trying to be very quiet is a strain. Therefore, he recommends that people move periodically in order to keep the blood flowing and the energy level up.

As always, moderation is the answer: strive for a reduction of unnecessary steps but have an office environment in which people are free to move about, be relaxed, and speak without disturbing others.

Type and arrangement of desks

The next step in creating a time efficient office is to look at the type and arrangement of desks. The typewriter and desk are the two basic tools of the educational office employee. As such they may contribute to or detract from efficient time management. Some factors to consider:

Desks should not face the window. The changing light caused by the movement of the sun and the reflection of the trees and shrubs causes the pupils of the eyes to dilate and contract frequently, thus resulting in increased eye strain.

Desk tops should be light tan with a nongloss finish. Dark colors absorb the light and cause eye strain. Shiny light colors reflect the light into the face and also create eye strain. Unfortunately, office staff members often find it convenient to cover desk tops with clear plastic and then place underneath it important information such as bell schedules, telephone numbers, and emergency information. Although this is efficient, it does create eye strain. Those two factors must be weighed.

Placing desks in the right location and providing a light tan cover is not enough. The next step is to look at the desk itself. The desk should be standard size—the secretary should be able to reach the far corners of it without standing up. Large executive desks cause extra stretching and fatigue. If additional space is needed, try placing a table either on one side or immediately behind the desk. This will provide additional working surface yet be within access of the chair.

Many chairs create fatigue in the office employee because they are either too high or too low or have the back support in the wrong place. Be sure that your chair fits your body structure.

Lighting and color of wall paint

How can the color of the walls affect time management? It does so in a subtle but substantial way. According to *Administrative Office Management,* production can improve 15 to 30 percent when colors are selected scientifically. If educational office staff members are involved in the selection of the colors for the office, it is important that they be aware of the significance of color. For instance, sunlight takes on different color hues depending on the direction of the light.

Sunlight from the north has a blue tinge
Sunlight from the east has a white tinge
Sunlight from the south has a yellow tinge
Sunlight from the west has an orange tinge

How can this be helpful? For example, a room in a warm climate with windows facing west receives the late afternoon sun (with an orange tinge), so it should be painted in a blue or green color to give the illusion of coolness.

Viewing office management as a component of efficient time management often provides the incentive to do something about the environment.

FILING

A chapter on time management would not be complete without a section devoted to the most disliked responsibility of the educational office staff, filing. The reason it is included in this chapter is that a great deal of time and energy is expended putting off the task and then having to wade through reams of papers and reports to catch up. Planning and developing an efficient method will help eliminate the problem—it may never change it into a cherished duty, but it will lessen the time spent on it.

An outstanding resource for virtually every educational office is *File It Right and Find It,* published by the National Association of Educational Office Personnel. This practical approach to filing deals with subject filing in terms of topics commonly found in school and administrative offices. The "File It Right" system, coupled with a color coding system, will help even the largest filing and records management setup.

Yet converting to the "File It Right" system does not always solve the filing dilemma. Since filing is so disliked by office staff, people often avoid the task. The only thing worse than filing is to organize and file an accumulation of material or to try to find one piece of correspondence in a sea of paper.

Analyzing why this is a universally disliked task is not difficult: educational office employees are people-oriented rather than filing-oriented. People respond to being helped and provide a reward system through their gratitude. Paper does not respond to people, so material is approached with a universal lack of enthusiasm.

When the dreaded filing day finally occurs, probably half the stack is tossed into the wastepaper basket. According to a concept called the Pareto Principle, fully 80 percent of the material in files is never needed. This is why secretaries are advised not to correct carbon copies of letters (if they are not using a duplicating machine): there is an 80 percent chance they will never have to retrieve the letter. Now we are not suggesting that 80 percent of the papers waiting to be filed should be discarded. Many are needed for reference or historical value. What we are suggesting is a timesaving method to dispose of the paper load and provide a functional effective method of records management.

Since material to be filed falls into several categories, we shall address each segment separately.

LETTERS AND MEMOS (OUTGOING)

Make two copies of letters and memos. Mark one for the file folder and, if possible, file immediately. If this is not possible, mark it with the proper title and place in a folder or tray for filing.

The second copy should be punched and placed alphabetically in a three-ring binder which has A through Z separators. The binder should be used to keep a daily file of correspondence for six months. When material from it is discarded, the other copy remains in the permanent file.

The daily file is a time-saver, since most copies of correspondence are referred to shortly after being mailed. Additionally, administrators soon become proficient in using the daily file and can look for copies when the secretary is out of the office.

INCOMING MATERIAL

School offices are inundated with letters, memos, policy bulletins, and rules. The first step in dealing with the incoming material is to organize it into the following groups:

Incoming letters from outside sources
Incoming letters and memos from school sources
Memos, bulletins, and policy statements
Advertisements

Handling incoming mail is the key to filing efficiency and time management. If possible, handle it only once. Divide the mail into the four categories. Mark the material for file folders. If extra copies of bulletins come in, circulate them to those who require the information and discard or return the extras.

Read school district policies for retention dates. Many items are meant to be read and discarded. File a paper only if it has lasting value. Filing cabinets are expensive. If the Pareto Principle is correct, 80 percent of the material in the files could be eliminated, and fewer cabinets purchased. Think of the savings.

By establishing a procedure for handling and marking incoming mail, you can greatly reduce the volume of filing. What must be filed is organized and stacked in chronological order, last date on top, waiting to be filed.

Theoretically, office staff should file daily or weekly. But if this is impossible, at least the filed material is organized in separate piles in reverse chronological order. If something needed is still awaiting filing, only one of the stacks need be handled.

Whatever the filing system used, all members of the staff, administrative and clerical, should be aware of the way the system is organized. Develop a one-page outline describing the system you are using and the general categories. This should be filed in the job procedure manual. Additionally, an index of each file drawer should be placed in the front so that instead of going through each file, a person seeking a piece of material need only glance at the index page.

For very complex systems, develop a 3 × 5 index card system listing major categories as well as cross-filing information. The worst thing that can happen to an office is to have someone come in, reorganize the files, and then leave, with no history of where things are filed.

No matter how well organized the system is, or how well informed the staff is, filing is probably never destined to be a high priority for the educational office employee who is people-oriented. Yet, the educational office does need a system of information retrieval that works efficiently. Perhaps the answer is to acknowledge the person who takes the time to file. If people were given the same positive feedback for filing as they are for helping others, perhaps even filing would become enjoyable.

SUMMARY

No one has the ability to confer time on others. No one has more time than any other person. Therefore, it is up to the individual to make the best use of the time allotted.

For the educational office staff, with constant interruptions and demands on time, the efficient use of time becomes dependent on

being aware of personal styles and needs
planning, determining priorities, and projecting
analyzing the office for efficiency
realizing that filing is not fun, but it can be efficient
developing a sense of humor.

In reality, despite every measure taken, there are days when nothing works, the flu bug hits the student body, the district office needs immediate information, and the fire alarm malfunctions, turning all the students out on the school grounds. It is on days such as these that the best thing to do is to follow the adage of the National Association of Educational Office Personnel: "Don't panic, adjust."

Bibliography

File It Right and Find It. Arlington, Va.: National Association of Educational Secretaries, 1977.

Lakein, Alan. *How to Get Control out of Your Time and Your Life.* New York: Peter H. Wyden, Inc., 1973.

MacKenzie, R. Alec. *The Time Trap.* New York: American Management Association, 1972.

Morehouse, Lawrence E., and Gross, Leonard. *Maximum Performance.* New York: Simon and Schuster, 1977.

Neuner, John J. W., et al. *Administrative Office Management.* Cincinnati, Ohio: South-Western Publishing Company, 1973.

Steere, Ralph E., Jr. *Office Work Simplification.* Englewood Cliffs, N.J.: Prentice-Hall, 1963.

Take Time to Plan: An Anthology for Educational Office Personnel. Arlington, Va.: National Association of Educational Secretaries, 1977.

Chapter 11

Career Development: A Plan
for Upward Mobility

We firmly believe that the complexity of the responsibilities and role of the educational office employee is unique. The volume and variety of interaction with people who enter the office is greater than that encountered by other office staffs. The accomplished educational secretary becomes proficient in such a variety of areas that career development is a natural extension of the position.

The educational office employee who wishes to pursue advanced career opportunities has acquired the skills to make the transition easily. This chapter will be devoted to helping those individuals to reflect on past and present knowledge, skills, and abilities in order to build for the job of the future.

Although we see this chapter as a natural progression, we also realize that some secretaries do not wish to pursue career development. The present job is challenging, the rewards are significant, and the satisfaction is there. Therefore, we ask the reader to use this chapter only if timing is appropriate.

The fundamental premise on which the career development field is based is that people should project into the future and develop goals, objectives, and plans to help them achieve these goals and objectives.

It sounds simple enough. Yet, as with any apparently simple concept, the achievement of the plan may be exceedingly difficult. Why? Basically, it is because many people (and women especially) have never viewed working as a life-long activity. It was generally seen as a transitory activity to end when conditions changed or improved. However, for most people, whether they recognize it or not, working is not a temporary activity. It is a life-long commitment which should be explored in order to make the commitment as meaningful as possible.

To aid the reader on this journey of exploration and expansion, we must look to the past and the present. Figure 11-1 is the first step in the journey. Please take your time when filling it out. Do not restrict your answers. Respond openly and spontaneously. You can use the in-

Figure 11–1   Career Exploration Survey

1. I became an educational office employee because _____

_____

_____

2. The educational requirements for my job are _____

_____

_____

3. The reason(s) I like my job is/are _____

_____

_____

4. The reason(s) I dislike my job is/are _____

_____

_____

5. The most rewarding aspects of my job are _____

_____

_____

6. The most unrewarding aspects of my job are _____

_____

_____

7. The things I do best that I like are _____

_____

_____

Figure 11–1 (*continued*)

8. The things I do best that I do not like are _____

_____

_____

9. The things I do not do well but would like to do better are _____

_____

_____

10. The things I do not do well and have no desire to do better are __

_____

_____

11. If I were granted one wish for a job I would really love to do, it would be (let your fantasies soar, do not limit yourself) _____

_____

_____

formation throughout the chapter as you explore, evaluate, and develop career options.

Once you have completed the survey, review the answers. Were there any surprises? Have you ever thought about the responsibilities you really enjoy and those you dislike? Have you ever separated the tasks you do well and those you do not? And have you ever considered why you do some jobs well, but do not really like them, and do not do some well, but would like to?

The survey can provide valuable information about you, information to help you decide on your career options.

In the past, career development was often a hit or miss technique. Today, career planning incorporates systematic strategies and plans with a great deal of structure. This is the beginning of your journey into the future; it should give you greater insight into what you do best and where you want to use your energies in the quest for career advancement.

This career development path will cover the following areas:

Comparing Individual and Organizational Values
Exploring Career Options
Detailing Assets and Assets to Be Developed
Developing a Roadmap to Career Success
Sharing Goals with Significant People in Your Life
Developing Résumés Which Support Career Goals
Preparing for Interviews
Evaluating Progress

COMPARING INDIVIDUAL AND ORGANIZATIONAL VALUES

The first step in developing a career development program is to explore life goals. There is no mystery to the reason: people find it difficult to put enthusiasm and energy into a career inconsistent with their sense of values and philosophy toward life. Generally, people who work in the educational field do find satisfaction in that environment. However, with the educational environment (or any other) come rewards and penalties. Therefore, as a first step in preparing a career plan, it is necessary to determine exactly what values are important to you and whether these values are reflected in potential work environments.

CAREER PLANNING STEP 1

Determine the priority of concepts listed in Figure 11-2. Space has been provided for you to add values which are not listed, but which you feel are important to you.

After you feel comfortable that the list represents your own sense of values, put the items in priority order. Only this time reflect on whether your values are demonstrated by the school or office where you work. If not, it may be necessary to explore your feelings. Can you live with the differences or is the disparity one that suggests a change in work environment is necessary? This may be a difficult decision, but it needs to be made before you move on to the next step.

If, in the process of making this comparison of values, you realize that the educational environment is not congruent with personal values, then the subsequent processes will provide guidance in seeking other avenues of employment. Perhaps, when faced with this difference, you will suddenly understand why, in the past, so many things seemed to create inner conflict.

Figure 11–2

	I value	My organization values
_____	being a leader	_____
_____	controlling others	_____
_____	becoming well known to others	_____
_____	having security and stability	_____
_____	making a great deal of money	_____
_____	enjoying what I do	_____
_____	having knowledge so that I am viewed as an authority	_____
_____	doing what I like, when I like	_____
_____	working with people who are as dedicated as I am to the goals of the organization.	_____
_____	_____	_____
_____	_____	_____
_____	_____	_____

The existence of a difference does not mean one must change jobs. Once you understand your feelings of uneasiness, you may be able to go forward and accept what heretofore had been an enigma. Whatever the decision, comparison of personal and organizational values is a necessary step on the path to career development.

EXPLORING CAREER OPTIONS

What do you want to be when you grow up? For many—especially educational office staff—this question has not been answered.

In the past, many who entered the field were at first parents involved with the PTA; when their children had grown, they turned a volunteer job into one with a salary. Often this transition occurred without planning and with the expectation that the job would be short-lived. Today, many who enter the field do so because the educational climate is appealing. Yet few really believe that they will be working most of their adult lives.

In 1979, more than 40 percent of the work force was composed of women.[1] Nine out of ten women will work some time in their life.

---

[1] Bureau of Labor Statistics.

Therefore, it is not premature or inappropriate to project one-, three-and five-year goals. The reality is that most people will be working a great part of their lifetime.

The goals one sets must be achievable and measurable, with a time setting and a method of evaluation. However, nothing prohibits the goal setter from fantasizing about a career. In fact, through fantasizing, goal setters have the opportunity to explore their inner selves and find out what job would be the most satisfying for them. People find it easier to attain goals providing inner satisfaction. The fantasy process helps individuals to explore their ultimate dreams in jobs.

However, before we move on to career fantasies, let's look at career realities.

CAREER PLANNING STEP 2

Research jobs available to you in your district and community. This can be done through personnel offices, listings of job descriptions, and local employment advertisements.

If a local industry has appeal, obtain a copy of the prospectus and product information. These provide a great deal of information on the jobs available. If this fails, try phone calls. Often the personnel director will willingly give an overview of the positions available. After all, some-one who takes the time to do this calling demonstrates motivation and initiative, qualities sought by employers.

For the purpose of this chapter, we will focus on job descriptions generally available from educational personnel offices.

Review all descriptions for jobs that in any way appeal to you. Call people who currently hold these positions and find out how they prepared for the job.

After reviewing the information, proceed to the next step: the fantasy.

CAREER PLANNING STEP 3

Read this segment through and then complete the exercise.

Close your eyes and visualize yourself in five years. Let the vision unfold. What are you wearing? Where are you working? What are you doing? Who is reporting to whom?

As you view yourself, let your imagination soar. Watch yourself perform the responsibilities of the job.

After the mental activity is complete, quickly write down what you visualized on the Fantasy Goal Sheet (Figure 11–3). It is important to capture every nuance, every detail of the picture.

Figure 11–3   Fantasy Goal Sheet

What I was doing _____

_____

People who were there with me _____

_____

My role in the group _____

_____

The setting _____

I was wearing _____

_____

CAREER PLANNING STEP 4

The next step is to analyze what your fantasy has revealed.

What job did you picture yourself performing?
Is it achievable in five years?
If not, can it be amended to be achievable?

Ask yourself the following questions:

Do I need certain skills to achieve the goal?
Can I get the special training needed?
Do I need additional education?
Will the job be available in five years?

The only thing worse than having no career goal is having one you cannot possibly reach. If you find the position you desire is truly impossible, it is time to stop and take a midcourse correction. Perhaps the goal will take more like ten years to achieve and some interim steps are in order. Or perhaps a slight detour can bring you to a job just as fulfilling and rewarding.

Return to the Career Exploration Survey (Figure 11–1) you prepared at the beginning of the chapter, looking especially at questions 5, 7, and 8. What do you really like to do? Does your fantasy support what you have written?

The rationale for becoming career and goal oriented is perhaps best expressed by Socrates: "If a man does not know to which port he is sailing, then no wind is favorable."

This concept is still sound. By exploring achievable five-year goals, the reader gains a sense of awareness, a sense of direction, and, most important, a sense of purpose.

DETAILING ASSETS AND ASSETS TO BE DEVELOPED

The wording of the title of this segment exemplifies the basic philosophy of career pathing and developing—optimism. As you know, the typical expression is "assets and liabilities." However, career development does not focus on the negative, but highlights the positive. The word "liabilities" suggests deficiencies. The phrase "assets to be developed" suggests a willingness and ability to learn and achieve.

Is this antics with semantics? We think not. The person who is successful in climbing the career ladder is the one who believes in herself or himself and is confident of achieving. Therefore, we feel use of the words "assets to be developed" and the acceptance of the concept are fundamental to the successful completion of the plan.

CAREER PLANNING STEP 5

Assets and Assets to Be Developed suggest a balance sheet concept. Therefore in this career planning step, we recommend using a form similar to Figure 11-4.

On the left side, list all skills, knowledge, and abilities you possess. Do not limit yourself to those used solely on the job. Include skills used in volunteer organizations, social clubs, and at home. A welcome trend in the workplace is the acceptance of all job experiences, whether developed in a paying or a nonpaying environment. The trick is to express these skills in the right way—an area we will soon discuss.

On the right side, list the Assets to Be Developed. Included should be areas in which you are now performing, but feel you could do better. Also include skills you will need to achieve your five-year goal. Refer to the Fantasy Goal Sheet (Figure 11-3). What do you need to do and learn to compete for the position? In addition, review the Career Exploration Survey (Figure 11-1) to incorporate skills mentioned as well as areas needing development.

Figure 11–4

Assets	Assets to Be Developed

Perhaps you may need to list assertiveness training because the position requires proficiency in communication skills. Or perhaps you feel you must make a concerted effort to enlist the aid and support of the administrator in charge.

Total honesty and openness are at this point essential. No one will see the sheet. Level with yourself.

Realistically formulated Assets to Be Developed should fall into three categories:

Skills acquirable on the job

Knowledge obtainable in local schools and colleges

Training falling under the "I know I need to learn but cannot figure out where to get the training" category.

Now we will take them one at a time.

Skills acquirable on the job. Review your responsibilities and those of your administrator. Determine if there are any your administrator performs for which you can assume responsibility. This accomplishes two things: you lighten your administrator's work load and you have the opportunity to develop a new skill on the job. Acquiring budget experience is an example. Budget is generally the responsibility of the administrator, but can be delegated.

Knowledge obtainable in local schools and colleges. Do not restrict yourself to classes geared to office personnel. It is often possible to audit classes geared for teachers and administrators without enrolling for credit. Check with the local university to determine policies. Additionally, do not overlook conferences and workshops. Contact local education office employee associations, the National Association of Educational Office Personnel, and the National Secretaries Association for workshops in your area.

Training falling under the "I need to learn but can't figure out where to get the training" category. Where can you gain experience in specific skills when there are no classes available and the present job does not offer any opportunity to learn them? Here imagination is your best asset. Volunteer work for professional and philanthropic organizations can provide the needed experience. Generally organizations relying on the services of volunteers need the same skills and knowledge used in school settings and administrative offices. By offering your services free to perform specific tasks (if training is provided) you may open doors heretofore closed. Additionally, since the position is not paid, there is an opportunity to learn without the pressures normally experienced on a paying job. Have you ever heard of a volunteer's being fired?

The opportunities abound:

Boy and Girl Scout groups
Professional associations
Religious organizations.

In addition, certain associations provide specific skill training:

Toastmistress Club
Toastmasters Club

The way you approach the Assets to Be Developed column is often an indicator of how you feel about reaching career goals. If you lack the enthusiasm to explore ways of achieving these skills, you might reconsider whether the position you *think* you want is really the job you *do* want. If this seems to be the problem, go back to your Career Exploration Survey and Fantasy Goal Sheet. Perhaps they need additional analysis.

However, if this last activity instilled in you the enthusiasm and energy to move on to the next step, then it is time to be developing a roadmap to career success.

DEVELOPING A ROADMAP TO CAREER SUCCESS

You are well on your way—the foundation of planning career expansion is almost complete. The next step is to develop step-by-step procedures with a projected time frame.

CAREER PLANNING STEP 6

It is now time to transfer the career information you have developed to the Goal Projection Activity Sheet (see Figure 11-5).

The first step is to list your current position and the assets you possess.

Figure 11–5   Goal Projection Activity Sheet

Present Position	One-Year Goal	Three-Year Goal	Five-Year Goal
Skills	HAVE	HAVE	HAVE
	NEED	NEED	NEED
Knowledge	HAVE	HAVE	HAVE
	NEED	NEED	NEED
Technical Abilities	HAVE	HAVE	HAVE
	NEED	NEED	NEED
Education	HAVE	HAVE	HAVE
	NEED	NEED	NEED

Skills, e.g., communication

Knowledge, e.g., Board of Education rules

Technical abilities, e.g., typing, stenography

Education, e.g., High school graduation, College, classes in accounting

Next move to the five-year goal. What skill level must you attain to fulfill this expectation? Using the information you have extracted from interviewing people in the field and studying job descriptions, fill in this area as completely as possible.

The next step is to develop one- and three-year goals that will lead to the attainment of the five-year goal. Figure 11-4 on Assets and Assets to Be Developed will be of assistance in projecting these needs.

Notice that Figure 11-5 has places to list the skills, knowledge, technical abilities, and education you already have that meet the requirements for these projected goals. As we have stressed repeatedly, the educational office staff receives training in such a multitude of responsibilities that one can easily move upward.

It is essential to project one- and three-year goals. Without the reward of short-term achievements, people often lose interest in long-range efforts. Moreover, as you reach the interim goals, you can reexamine the long-term projection to determine if the career goal is still on target. Nothing is more discouraging than attaining a goal that has ceased to be meaningful or important. Midcourse corrections are not uncommon and may well be essential to career satisfaction.

With the completion of the Goal Projection Activity Sheet, it is time to move on to the next step—sharing your goals with significant people in your life.

BEING A PART OF A PERSON'S SUCCESS

Do you view involving another as placing a burden on that person or sharing a gift? Or, if this person happens to be an administrator, do you feel that sharing career goals with him or her poses a threat? Do you worry that he or she will be angry and punitive? In recent years, as more opportunities have become available to the office staff, sharing goals with administrators has been seen as risky.

Yet, upon closer examination, the reason for an administrator's anger (if it does occur) is generally that he or she has not been informed of the subordinate's plans until changes were about to be made. A school secretary who wanted to leave would scout the area, make the arrangements, and then guiltily share the information with the administrator. Any anger on the part of the administrator was translated to mean that he or she did not want the subordinate to leave the job. More often than not, the annoyance stemmed from being the last person to know.

On the other hand, sharing goals involves other people in your success—and their contributions can be significant.

SHARING GOALS

Have you ever struggled with a burdensome task by yourself, wishing you had help but reluctant to ask? Then along came someone who offered a helping hand and the job was finished in no time?

Two significant things happened:

1. You felt that you were not out there alone. In other words, someone cared and you had a support network.
2. The other person went away feeling satisfaction for helping someone else and being part of the individual's success.

These concepts—not feeling alone and being part of a person's success—play important roles in achieving career success.

CAREER PLANNING STEP 7

Develop plans to share career goals with administrators, peers, and family.

SUPPORT NETWORKS

Sharing career goals with others creates a support network—people who can be called on to listen, help, and provide input. There are times when choices must be made. Discussing them with others provides different viewpoints and more information on which to make the choice. A job that may, on the surface, seem either undesirable or very attractive may look very different from someone else's vantage point. You need the benefit of these perceptions to make intelligent choices.

SIGNIFICANT PEOPLE IN YOUR LIFE

The people around you are perfect candidates both to provide a support network and to be part of your success.: administrators, peers, and family.

Administrative Support   Receiving support from an administrator who believes you have the ability to do a particular job may sway you to accept a position you really wanted but were uncertain you could perform properly. In addition, on many occasions the attainment of career goals is dependent on learning more advanced skills that can be acquired at your present position. If you share your needs with the administrator, he or she may create opportunities to help you perfect these skills. This person has become part of the support network working to help you achieve.

It is often a short step

from	to
maintaining bookkeeping records	preparing the budget
providing on-the-job training	developing a training manual and implementing a training program
maintaining files	developing and maintaining a records management procedure

With your knowledge of your present job and the one you aspire to, you can provide a more detailed list. The administrator who knows your goals and is part of your support network can often provide the training opportunities you need to learn the necessary skills to achieve the position.

In sum, making the administrator part of your success team can benefit you because he or she may then

provide you with opportunities to expand and enhance your skills

support your endeavors with colleagues

write referrals validating your goals and accomplishments.

And the rewards go both ways. By involving the administrator you permit him or her to

become aware that office staff have career aspirations

realize that the school office provides valuable experiences leading to upward mobility

be a significant contributor to your success. In other words, "I knew her when."

Peer Support   There will come a time when the whole notion of career development and upward mobility will appear to you as the most ridiculous plan you ever had. Generally it is the day when the phones are the busiest, the work is the heaviest, and the pressure is the greatest. At this point you may think learning another job or getting a more responsible position is the last thing you need. Do not despair.

If you have shared your goals with the office staff team you will have a built-in support group to help you over the rough days. Remember, you are an example to them, indicating that they too can move ahead. They have a vested interest in your success. Mutual reliance is one of the soundest ways of creating success for all involved.

Often, the reason peers who are left behind feel abandoned is because no communication takes place between the office staff member who leaves and those who are left behind.

The reverse of "She just stayed till she learned what she could—and then she left" is "She shared her goals with me. This job provided her with the training to move ahead and I was glad to help. I am making my own plans now."

People resent being used, yet are delighted to be of help. The former involves exploiting; the latter involves sharing and communicating.

Family Support   It is difficult to calculate which group is needed more—one's administrators, peers, or family. Certainly the support of your home team is critical to your success. Having your family in there behind you will keep you from giving up on your goals.

Spouse and children can help with home responsibilities. More importantly, they can provide words of encouragement on those nights when staying at home to watch television sounds much more appealing than going to class.

Families who are involved can keep the most discouraged person on the road to success. Moreover, involvement gives the supporting family members satisfaction; they know how much their support has contributed to the achievement of the goal. This brings us to the second concept—being a part of a person's success.

Striving to achieve a career goal brings changes to the family—extra duties, less time with you, and concern over how you will change. Whether it is because you attend classes, expend more energy at work, are more tired, or travel longer distances, your family will experience some changes.

As with administrators and peers, the changes can be seen as an added burden with no rewards, or as an added responsibility with untold rewards. Generally the perception of the family will depend on the attitude of the person seeking the career change.

When family members must assume greater responsibilities for housework and chores, while contenting themselves with less time with the person, they can receive rewards through:

knowing that the person they are helping is seeking to achieve a better job with resultant financial rewards.

knowing that by helping the individual they are contributing to the successful attainment of a goal.

seeing their contribution enhance the individual's abilities and self-esteem as the person achieves new successes.

receiving acknowledgment of their contribution through the achievement of the person.

becoming aware of how much more capable each family member is than they had previously thought.

Expanded career options for the parents play significant roles in the aspirations of the children. Just the parent's activity of striving and achieving is a powerful message to the children.

The family can be enriched from the day the person set his or her sights on an expanded career goal. Of course, the view of an optimist is a fundamental component of career planning and goal achieving.

DEVELOPING RÉSUMÉS WHICH SUPPORT CAREER GOALS

The development of the résumé culminates the many career development and planning activities. In essence, the résumé is an advertisement for you, highlighting the areas of expertise you delineated in prior activities. Additionally, it is a way of concealing those areas not supportive of your career quest. "Best foot forward" is the motto—there is no point in focusing on areas of deficiency. The résumé gives you an opportunity to highlight strengths while camouflaging weaknesses.

The art of résumé writing has been perfected in recent years. Remember, résumés are not job applications—they are advertisements. Their purpose is to publicize special abilities and qualities which will create a positive influence on prospective employers. Therefore, not all experiences need be documented—only those which demonstrate your ability to perform the needed job skills.

This change in format makes it considerably easier to assemble material for the résumé. In the past, people were always in a quandry about which experiences to include and which to leave out. If you focus on the intended position and the needs of the prospective employer, the direction becomes clear. However, this focus on a particular position or set of duties often necessitates the preparation of more than one résumé. While time-consuming, this approach helps ensure success.

This new focus in writing comes as a boon to the educational office employee. In trying to make the move to a new position, the individual is often faced with stereotypes of what people think the individual does as opposed to what he or she really does. It is no longer necessary to enumerate typing and shorthand skills. If the position held was secretarial, this goes without saying. You should enumerate managerial functions you have performed (if appropriate). While we are not advocating lying, we do believe that stating clerical skills often influences the employer in a negative manner. This perception hinders the future employer from truly analyzing what the prospective employee can really do. Therefore, it is up to the individual to focus on the skills that are most important for the desired position.

Of course, if the position being sought is of a clerical or secretarial nature, including typing and stenographic skills is appropriate. It is when one is trying to move out of the secretarial field that those skills should not be mentioned. Focus instead on the managerial and analytical components of the present job.

Yet, just focusing on these skills is not enough. After you decide what to include, the next step is to look at how it should be included. Secretarial job descriptions often describe the position with words that do not convey the complexity of the work. Therefore, it is up to the individual to use powerful terms which more realistically describe responsibilities.

Typical Duties	*Action-oriented Words*
File and maintain records	Develop, implement, and maintain a record management system
Make appointments	Coordinate and maintain calendars
Meet the public and help answer questions	Maintain positive district image and disseminate information to the public
Meet deadlines	Plan and coordinate office functions to fulfill organizational timelines
Work with clerical staff	Train, supervise, and coordinate office staff.

The above list will help you focus on your own supervisory and managerial functions and state them in a more positive way. Action-oriented power words are simply a tool to help educational office employees cover more completely what they really do.

Using action-oriented words is just the beginning. Remember, the résumé makes a powerful statement about the writer.

It indicates knowledge of English and writing ability.

Is the writing parallel?
Is the grammar correct?
Is the writing specific and to the point?

It indicates motivation.

Have you been keeping current in the field by going to school?
Do you belong to professional associations to keep up with the state of your profession?

It indicates skills.

Are there erasures?
Is the format neat—did you leave margins?
Have you confined the information to one page?

It indicates flexibility.

Have you had a variety of experiences?
Have you worked at several schools or offices?

Your responses to these questions may indicate additional areas you wish to explore or develop.

The goal of résumés is to sell your abilities and capabilities. If the product (you) is not as desirable as it should be, it is time to augment your plans to encompass those areas needing improvement.

CAREER PLANNING STEP 8

Write and rewrite responsibilities, using action-oriented descriptions and highlighting strengths.

Develop résumés for specific jobs or positions.

Analyze your résumé for areas you wish to develop.

Ask your administrator to read your résumé. Will he or she support what you have written in a reference?

PREPARING FOR INTERVIEWS

Preparing for interviews should be approached in the same manner as the previous steps—with deliberation and planning.

Typically this step creates the most anxiety. If the prospect makes you feel as if there were butterflies in your stomach, then the answer is preparation: help those butterflies to fly in formation.

The way to prepare is to research.

1. Obtain a job description for the position you are seeking, if one is available. (You may have used one to develop your Assets and Assets to Be Developed.) If one is not available, go to the library and find out the typical duties of jobs in the category for which you are applying. Most libraries have several books listing occupational duties. If this does not work, call the person who currently has the job, if feasible. If all else fails, it may be necessary to wait for the interview to ask what qualities the interviewer is looking for. After all, the interviewer is just as interested in getting the right person for the job as you are. However, let's pursue using the job description.

2. Scan the description for typical duties and skills, knowledge, and abilities expected. Contrast these with the assets on your sheet and you will have an idea of how closely you fit the qualifications. Focus on the areas where you do not meet the qualifications. Can you substitute schooling or similar experiences for these requirements?

3. Practice going through the interview with a friend or family member. Have the person ask questions about the areas where you lack necessary experience. Practice responding with substitute activities. For example:

    You have had no experience in statistics, but have taken a class from the local college.

    You have had no experience in school budgeting but have taken full charge of the bookkeeping system at your church.

    You have not supervised a staff of office people but have led organizations and taught at a local adult school.

    Interviewers are looking for ability and flexibility. Demonstrate that you have those qualities.

4. Find out the mode of dress at the school or office where you will be interviewed. If the job is in industry, take time to visit the site before the interview to observe the dress code. Al-

though few places have written dress codes, they exist nonetheless. Observations will help you determine appropriate dress. Remember, clothing makes a statement about you before you have a chance to smile or respond to a question. Generally, being conservative is safe. However, if you are seeking a managerial position, try to determine how the managers dress. Select your wardrobe accordingly and then practice role playing again. Make sure the clothing is comfortable and conveys the image you wish to portray.

5. Prior to the interview, gather letters of recommendation, commendations, diplomas, and any other certificates or documents demonstrating your capability to perform the job. Carry them to the interview in a conservative folder or attaché case. Generally, at the end of interviews they ask if you wish to add anything. This may be the opportunity to share them. Remember, do not offer anything that does not support your mission.

6. The evening before the interview, assemble the clothing and letters of commendation, then get a good night's sleep.

7. Take a snack with you to the interview. If you find your interview is right before the break or lunchtime and your stomach threatens to rumble during the interview, step into the hall or the restroom and eat the snack. You will be nervous enough without worrying about a rumbling stomach.

8. Come prepared with a list of questions you wish to have answered. If, during the interview, you do not get the answers, and the interviewer gives you the opportunity to ask questions at the end, do so. Coming prepared indicates interest and initiative—both qualities that employers value.

9. About the interview: often stress questions or challenging questions are asked. Remember, the purpose of such questions is to test your reasoning and analytical powers under pressure. There is usually more than one correct answer.

10. If after a week you have not heard from the person who interviewed you, call and find out if the selection has been made. If it has (and you did not get the job), this will settle the issue. If it has not, this gives you an opportunity to show initiative and also answer any questions the interviewer may have.

11. Sending a thank-you letter is considered appropriate in some areas and taboo in others. Determine the policy in your community. Writing to add information to clarify a point may be helpful, while writing just to say "thank you" may convey a negative image. Check locally for the best method.

CAREER PLANNING STEP 9

Approach the interview with optimism. You have worked hard and this is your opportunity to demonstrate what you have learned.

Practice interviewing with friends.

Plan your wardrobe in advance and make sure it is appropriate and comfortable.

Picture yourself going through the interview. Mentally imagine the whole process. End with a feeling of success.

Enter the interview room with a feeling of success—you've certainly prepared well.

EVALUATING PROGRESS

Any career development program would be incomplete without an evaluation component. Because plans may take several years to complete, it is essential to build in a system to evaluate goals. What may seem appropriate one year may not be so the next because of many factors: family, finance, lifestyle. Additionally, goals that may seem attractive when viewed from afar often lose their luster when viewed from a closer and clearer perspective.

Therefore, approximately every six months, take stock of your progress, your feelings, and your future.

CAREER PLANNING STEP 10

Periodically take out the career development papers you have prepared and review them.

Career Exploration Survey
Fantasy Goal Sheet
Assets and Assets to Be Developed
Goal Projection Activity Sheet

First, consider the Career Exploration Survey. Are your answers essentially still the same? If they are not, are the changes significant? Jot down areas needing further exploration.

Have you added any new areas to those which you enjoy?

Have you discovered any areas that you were unaware you disliked when you first prepared the survey?

Have your perceptions of yourself changed?

Second, look at the Fantasy Goal Sheet.

Is your fantasy the same now?
If not, how has it changed?
Do the changes influence your ultimate goal?

Third, study the Assets and Assets to Be Developed.

Can you move anything from the assets to be developed column
to the assets column?
Do you need to add any new items to the assets to be developed?
If so, how are you planning to acquire these skills?
Can some of the assets to be developed be eliminated from the list?
Has your perception of your abilities improved?

Finally, review your goal statements.

Have you achieved any?
Will you be able to complete some goals sooner than you expected?
Are your goals still on target, or have they changed? As you get
closer to achieving them, have they lost any appeal?
Do you wish to change your goals? if so,
  Review
  Revise
  Revamp
  Eliminate.

Remember, you have developed these goals. They belong to you.
You have the right to change them.

SUMMARY

If you have taken the time to do all the activities in this chapter,
you may feel that career planning and development take a great deal of
time. This is a fair and accurate observation. However, look at the alternative—doing nothing.

Time passes quickly. With or without one-, three-, and five-year
goals, the time will pass. Those who have a plan will be able to

evaluate whether they have accomplished the goals.

decide where they want to be in another five years.

reflect on the skills they have acquired while striving to meet the goals.

Those who have not made a plan will

be unaware of whether they could have used the time differently.

face uncertainty as to their plans for the future.

Whether goal planning focused on job projecting or retirement planning, it included planning—and planning suggests control over one's destiny.

This approach to a career is consistent with the underlying premise of this handbook: the responsibilities of an educational office employee are complex and diverse. Additionally, the role requires people to exercise leadership qualities. The combination of responsibility and leadership and the opportunities to exercise them results in people who have the ability to plan and control their destinies.

Bibliography

Ford, George A., and Lippitt, Gordon L. *Planning Your Future: A Workshop for Personal Goal Setting*. LaJolla, Calif.: University Associates, 1976.

Hogberg, Janet, and Leider, Richard. *The Adventurers: Excursions in Life and Career Renewal*. Menlo Park, Calif.: Addison-Wesley, 1978.

Jongward, Dorothy, and Seyer, Philip. *Choosing Success: Transactional Analysis on the Job*. New York: Wiley, 1978.

Miller, Donald B. *Personal Vitality*. Menlo Park, Calif.: Addison-Wesley, 1978, book and workbook.

Schein, Edgar H. *Career Dynamics: Matching Individual and Organizational Needs*. Menlo Park, Calif.: Addison-Wesley, 1978.

Sweeney, R. Carol. *Transition: Secretary to Manager*. Chatsworth, Calif.: Strategies for Success, 1980.

Annotated Bibliography

Many resources were used in developing the material for this book. They are noted at the end of each chapter. However, some books were so helpful we decided to take these resources and highlight especially useful segments and in-depth coverage of various subjects.

Dyer, Wayne. *Your Erroneous Zones*. New York: Funk & Wagnalls, 1976.

The section on anger and the techniques cited may prove particularly helpful to the reader.

This book makes many people feel as if concerns and examples cited are his or hers alone. It is very easy to relate to many of the situations described—which is probably why it was and is such a popular book.

Ferguson, Donald, et al. *Making the Wheels Go Round in School Public Relations*. Arlington, Va.: National Schools Public Relations Association, 1975.

This pamphlet contains excellent suggestions and techniques to implement a positive public relations climate in the office.

File It Right and Find It. Arlington, Va.: National Association of Educational Secretaries, 1977.

This pamphlet deals specifically with filing in school offices and administrative offices. It provides a comprehensive, practical, effective method of filing. A usually complicated subject is made incredibly easy.

Ford, George A., and Lippitt, Gordon L. *Planning Your Future*. La Jolla, Calif.: University Associates, 1972.

A comprehensive, practical workbook for the person who wishes an in-depth approach to life and career planning. Many of the exercises help the reader to explore personal values and how they influence or should influence the choice of profession.

Fox, Robert S. et al. *School Climate Improvement: A Challenge to The School Administrator*. Bloomington, In.: Phi Delta Kappa, 1973.

This book contains excellent techniques on improving school climate. Although focused and developed for the administrator, the techniques and surveys have application in the school office.

Gordon, Thomas. *Leader Effectiveness Training.* New York: Peter H. Wyden, Inc., 1977.

Dr. *Gordon, well known for* Teacher Effectiveness Training *and* Parent Effectiveness Training, *has applied the same techniques in his new book. This is a comprehensive book dealing with the complexities of interpersonal communications and the techniques to facilitate effective communication.*

Guidelines for Equal Treatment of the Sexes in McGraw-Hill Book Company Publications. New York: McGraw-Hill.

This publication can help office staff to become aware of sex stereotyping in textbooks. Additionally, the styles recommended serve as examples of non-sexist writing and can be applied to written communications for school and community.

Hersey, Paul, and Blanchard, Kenneth H. *Management of Organizational Behavior Utilizing Human Resources,* 3rd ed. Englewood Cliffs, N.J.: Prentice-Hall, 1977.

This book provides an overview of motivation techniques and then develops techniques for the supervisor to use. The content leans heavily on the instrument LEAD. Of special note is the authors' approach to supervision: looking at the needs of subordinates, not supervisors.

Jones, John E., and Pfeiffer, J. William. *Annual Handbooks for Group Facilitators.* La Jolla, Calif.: University Associates, 1972–1979.

The handbooks are issued yearly and contain a comprehensive approach to group process activities and instrumentation, theory, and resources. Many of the articles cited at the end of chapters came from this series.

Lakein, Alan. *How to Get Control out of Your Time and Your Life.* New York: Peter H. Wyden, Inc., 1973.

If you want to purchase just one time management book, this should be the one. Available in softback (Signet Books) it provides practical, realistic approaches to time management. Of special note is Chapter 10, Tasks Better Left Undone.

Mackenzie, R. Alec. *The Time Trap.* New York: AMACOM, 1972.

The chapter "Working with Your Secretary" has some excellent suggestions. Although generally the book focuses on the secretary-boss relationship found in industry rather than the service-to-many role of the school secretary, many of the suggestions can be adapted.

Marks, James R.; Stoops, Emery; and King-Stoops, Joyce. *Handbook of Educational Supervision: A Guide for the Practitioner.* Boston: Allyn and Bacon, 1971.

This book is one of the few developed for administrators. It also has a substantial section on classified personnel. It provides a clear, comprehensive overview of the delineation of responsibilities of support staff and techniques for full utilization of staff.

Neuner, John J. W., et al. *Administrative Office Management,* 6th ed. Cincinnati, Ohio: South-Western Publishing Co., 1972.

The material in this book provides a comprehensive survey of the most acceptable and effective methods and practices of office administration. Covered are areas such as furniture and equipment, automation, the office environment, human relations, and work flow. Of special note is the concept of color, sound, and light and their influence on morale and productivity.

Owens, Robert G. *Organizational Behavior in Schools.* Englewood Cliffs, N. J.: Prentice-Hall, 1970.

Although aimed at the administrative staff, the chapters on organizational climate, interpersonal relations, and organizational behavior have relevance to the educational office staff. These chapters help to place the school office in the organizational structure.

Robert, Marc. *School Morale, The Human Dimension.* Niles, Ill.: Argus Communications, 1976.

Many of the concepts, although focused on teachers and administrators, apply to the school office. Additionally, the personal surveys and checklists are relevant to support personnel.

Rutherford, Robert D. *Administrative Time Power.* Austin, Texas: Keneric Publishing Co., 1978.

This is a fast-reading, energetic book with innovative approaches. The chapter on Working Relations is thorough and thought-provoking; it is well worth the time and well worth sharing with the administrative staff.

Sabin, William A. *The Gregg Reference Manual,* 5th ed. New York: McGraw-Hill, 1977.

The Gregg Reference Manual is intended for anyone who writes, transcribes, or types. It presents the basic rules for virtually every piece of business writing. If the school staff were limited to only one resource book, this should be the one. Of note is the section dealing with sexism in language. It provides techniques to answer many of the most common problems in that area.

Schmuck, Richard A., et al. *The Second Handbook of Organization Development in Schools.* Palo Alto, Calif.: Mayfield Publishing Co., 1977.

This is an outstanding resource for an office employee who wishes to develop facilitating techniques to use in the school office. The activities in dealing with communication and conflict are well worth reading and provide techniques to open up and facilitate communication.

Steere, Ralph E., Jr. *Office Work Simplification.* New York: Prentice-Hall, 1963

This book provides a detailed step-by-step plan to simplify office work flow. Although the detail may be more than needed for small offices, the procedures enumerated would be helpful to a large office complex.

Stewart, Marie M., et al. *Business English and Communication,* 4th ed. New York: McGraw-Hill, 1972.

    Along with covering the principles of grammar, vocabulary building, and writing techniques, this book has "Quick Tricks" throughout the book giving the reader easy ways to remember complicated rules. Additionally, the authors deal effectively with the psychology of human behavior as it affects written and oral communication. A workbook is available.

Sweeney, R. Carol. *Transition: Secretary to Manager.* Chatsworth, Calif.: Strategies for Success, 1980.

    A comprehensive step-by-step approach for the secretary who wishes to capitalize on his or her skills, knowledge, and abilities to make the move into management.

Take Time to Plan: An Anthology for Educational Office Personnel. Arlington, Va.: National Association of Educational Secretaries, 1977.

    This book contains a comprehensive series of articles written by educational office personnel who have expertise in a variety of subjects. The subjects include communication, organization, self-worth, and career planning.

Index